To GARY REEDY
Best Wishes

A BAD DUCK HUNT

101 EXCUSES FOR EVERY UNFORTUNATE SITUATION

By Michael Terry
With Illustrations by Jerry Johnson

To get a copy of your favorite Jerry Johnson cartoon—an original signed and numbered print—or to order a bound copy of all the cartoons in book form, visit us at www.coldtreepress.com.

To the Luther Terrys in my life:

*My brother, Luther Leonidas Terry, Jr., with whom I shared
some great hunts on New Jersey's Barnegat Bay and
Luther Leonidas Terry III, with whom I hope to hunt . . .
in a few more years.*

*My son, Luther Durham Terry, who conspired with me to
conceive this wacky subject and whose great zest for the
outdoors—and life in general—are a continuing source
of inspiration to me.*

*My late father, Dr. Luther Leonidas Terry, world famous
physician who never forgot his Red Level, Alabama roots.
His wit, professionalism and dedication to the healing arts
will not soon be forgotten. My hunting trips with Dad were
not frequent, but each was memorable and cherished.*

Table of Contents

Acknowlegements

Our good friend Patty tells of her husband proposing, presenting a multi-carat diamond ring, dropping to one knee, staring wistfully into her eyes, asking for her hand. She was in the middle of whispering something like "Oh, yes, darling . . ." when he suddenly cut her off, blurting out, "Oh, by the way, you won't see me during duck season." Better to get reality on the table early in a relationship, than her wonder why you're setting the alarm clock for 3:00 a.m. when the weather starts getting cold.

While hunting seasons vary, recent years have seen seasons of up to sixty days. For those without calculators, the duck hunting season can be 17% of the total year. For some winsome brides, this is a heck of a lot of time. For the inveterate duck hunter, it is not nearly enough.

Actually, serious hunters realize that, over the years, many spouses relish the "absence makes the heart grow fonder" feeling . . . the old passion for your presence degrading to, "How can I miss you if you won't go off hunting?"

A sure sign your spouse is tiring of your glowing presence, she drops subtle hints: "Hey, isn't it about time for you to move over to your duck club?" And this comes at a July 4th picnic.

When in Philadelphia, New York and San Francisco, I was a passionate duck hunter. Then, after moving to an area where there is a duck blind next to every Starbuck's, my time in the field lessened . . . though my spiritual interest never has. I don't know, but there's something about a time-consuming job, wife, small children, home ownership, and other niggling stuff conspiring to keep one out of a pair of chest waders.

This circuitously gets me to thanking my family, wife Joan, daughter Agnes, and son Luke, for their patience with (occasionally even interest in) my eccentricities. Luke shares, in part, my unconventional view of the world. From this common perspective—in this case, peculiarities characteristic of duck hunters—this book emerged. Through kaleidscopic lenses, Luke and I see humor in unusual places and situations. Grown men dressed up as weeds, sitting in sub-zero weather, trying to "trick" waterfowl with molded plastic ducks seems to some folk an odd form of behavior, whereas we think it's perfectly normal. Thanks, Luke, for helping me conceive the concept for this book.

Sledge Taylor and Ferrell Varner offered valuable input. I greatly appreciate Chuck Smith's generous encouragement and abundant support . . . and a duck hunt or two at his fabulous Arkansas club, featuring great meals, fine wine, and zero ducks. (Chuck gives you a picked, frozen duck or two when you're heading home, actually not a bad deal, when you think about it.) Mike Starnes' great friendship and keen sense of humor helped (and giving us seats to the 2005 Duck Stamp awards dinner at the great Brooks Museum in Memphis). Rusty Mather and Stillman McFadden offered good ideas and support. Patty Tripper gave valuable suggestions. As a guest of my friend Tim

Dudley, I learned about shooting the marshes of Virginia's Rappahannock River (and "blue" ducks).

Thanks also to Frank Jemison, Jr., hunting friend and gentleman, whose words are important, whether in the field, office, or over a Mexican dinner in South Texas. Fred Stuckey showed me the singular beauty of black ducks locking up in a remote, pristine New Jersey marsh. (Yes, New Jersy *has* pristine marshes.) Thanks to the Lockleys who farm rice near Birdeye, Arkansas, graciously allowing me to watch hundreds of thousands of snow geese ignore my decoys and laugh at my calling.

Take A Kid Hunting

A Special Note

As you wander through this book, you'll enjoy Jerry Johnson's enormous creativity and talent. Indeed, Jerry exudes talent. He's a great painter, individual, and friend whose character and art I wholly admire and respect. I appreciate his stowing his artist's ego to render these terrific cartoons.

"If it wasn't for all these drawings, I could be out hunting!"

A BAD DUCK HUNT

101 EXCUSES FOR EVERY UNFORTUNATE SITUATION

By Michael Terry
With Illustrations by Jerry Johnson

Introduction

his is about duck hunting, specifically, about those who pursue the sport with zeal, even in the face of uncompromising and abject defeat.

Every year, duck hunters purchase over one and one half million *Federal Migratory Bird Hunting and Conservation Stamps*—"duck stamps"[1]—and bag[2] over *sixteen million* ducks and geese.

Perhaps, fortunately, no one measures the number of ducks that get away. But it's a big, big number. As a matter of fact, next to the actual hunt, a duck hunter's favorite pastime is the creation and delivery of excuses for failure.

Today, we're long past flimsy, pusillanimous responses like, "Well, I *really* like *being outside* . . . appreciating the outdoors . . . reveling in nature's resplendent beauty . . . breathing in the rich, cool air of the woods and marsh . . . taking in the slow coming of the rosy-fingered dawn . . . and reflecting on the majesty of a soaring eagle or great blue heron fishing in solitude along the banks

---

[1] Over the past 40 years, ducks stamp sales have varied from 1.25 million to 2.35 million.
[2] Duck hunters employ a variety of synonyms and euphemisms for killing. The most common are 'harvest'. 'bag', and 'take', e.g. 'We *took* two ducks this morning.'

1

of a tranquil pond."[3,4]

Every duck hunter knows that kind of talk is, put nicely, *rare*. The actual case is more like, "What a terrible day! Up in the middle of the night, sleepy, freezing my butt off, wet and cold . . . and didn't get a duck all morning!" (For the sake of basic decency, we've gone light on blasphemy and profane expletives. The inspired reader should use his imagination and artfully spice the narrative with his own personal favorites.)

So, Americans shoot[5] sixteen million ducks a year . . . and miss millions more. Well, that's a lot of Mossy Oak; Browning and Winchester ordnance; Labrador and Chesapeake Bay retrievers; Bass Pro Shops and Cabela's excursions, and Ducks Unlimited auctions, dinners and donations.

And, ironically, half the hunting stuff we buy, well, it's manufactured in you-know-where . . . China. A nation where, paradoxically, they have the good sense to raise *pure white* Pekin ducks—decidedly easier to observe and decoy—plus, they keep *their* ducks in pens so you can get a nice fat one whenever you please, (none of this silly 'into the woods' stuff, please!) albeit, perhaps with a little case of avian flu.

Only the true hunter revels in the relentless pursuit of water-

---

[3] "As I became older, I changed from an avid hunter to being satisfied with enjoying the diversity of wildlife in the marsh." Manager, Gray Lodge Refuge, California. 1947.

[4] "The black and angry clouds, ice fields, strange sounds in the woods and swiftly moving vistas of the ever-changing, restless river made up an effect which will not soon pass. It was novel, glorious, boating with the mercury below zero, the river narrowing slowly. Would I change my uneasy seat in this winter panorama to hunt other game on foot or play any fish. By no means. Such fascination I have never known." *American Duck Shooting* by George Bird Grinnell, Field & Stream Publishing, 1901. p. 345.

[5] Apparently, the official U.S. Government term for killing is 'harvest'. Hence, 'The Migratory Bird Harvest Information Program was created by the U.S. Fish and Wildlife Service to develop estimates of the total number of migratory birds harvested. These estimates give biologists information to make decisions concerning hunting seasons, bag limits, and population management.' *(See www.fws.gov).*

fowl, synthesizing the pleasures of getting up at 2:30 am; trying to locate that long list of things to do and bring; loading up an SUV in the dark; driving an hour, two, or more; realizing in your groggy stupor that you picked up your son's size 8 hip waders by mistake and cramming your feet into them anyway; transferring a container load of material and equipment to a short, leaky, underpowered tin boat (with the assistance of a flashlight for which, on each of the past seven weekends, you promised yourself you'd get new batteries); motor (or, alternatively slog, in thigh-deep water) for three-quarters of a mile, forty-five minutes to an already-occupied blind; forget your lunch; spill your coffee; drop your gun in the water; spend a half hour untangling decoys . . . all this while the juggernaut of the sun races up over the horizon faster than you can get set up . . . while you're climbing into your blind with your gun unloaded, getting buzzed by a few dozen ducks, none close enough or slow enough to hit; then sitting motionless for the next few hours in the bitter cold; finally gathering up all the accoutrements, apparatuses, appurtenances, appliances and armament . . . and dutifully motoring (or slogging) back homeward in an dreary exercise of the same process, except in reverse.

In some diabolical way, duck hunting is like golf[6]: a time consuming, expensive, frustrating, masochistic experience, all carried out with understanding and prevaricating friends. The major difference is that in duck hunting you do this under glacial[7]

[6] The National Institutes of Health (NIH) Center for Avian Adventure Related Mental Health, Disease and Personality Disorders (CAARMHDPD) reports that self-inflicted harm among individuals who both hunt ducks and play golf is 12.3 times the national average. See *"Do They Hate Themselves, or Love the Sport That Much? A Comparative Study and Failure in Golfers and Duck Hunters and Related Mental and Physical Afflictions"*; NIH Press, Bethesda, Maryland, 2002.

[7] 'Glacial' has double meaning in duck hunting, applying to the meteorological experience (i.e. freezing cold) and also to the pace of the 'activity', e.g. "We've been sitting for six hours and haven't seen a duck. But I *have* counted 3,328 red-winged blackbirds!"

conditions, getting soaked, without a beer cart in sight.

But, the most revered element is explaining, usually through gritted teeth, that the "experience" is "all that really matters anyway", trying desperately to sound like you mean it.

"Well, we didn't get any shots, see any ducks, we froze half to death, but we had a *great* time!" No wonder the word *apologeia* comes from the Greek meaning, "a defense of the faith."

And the most cherished, indeed indispensable, element of the endeavor is the inevitable explanation[8] of why the hunt was 'unsuccessful', at least in terms of bringing home any dead fowl, presumably the purpose for this passionate quest in the first place.

If you've spent enough time duck hunting (or just trading lies with duck hunters), you've heard every conceivable excuse . . . oops, *explanation* . . . for the paucity of meat on the table. The reasoning isn't necessarily false, or even 'enhanced'. It's just that the breadth and depth of each 'I-got-skunked' account differs in some slight way . . . but never lacks the basic elements of feasibility.

The Institute for the Study of Duck Hunters Experiencing Significant Cognitive Separation from Reality[9] studies the 'Duck Hunter Failure Syndrome'. The Institute's conclusion: there are three simple explanations for bad hunts:

1. "There were *no ducks anywhere* . . . at least as far was we could see. They must be *extinct* . . .

2. "There *were* ducks, but they weren't where we were."[10]

---

[8] Remember, the recounting of chronic failure is never an '*excuse*', always an '*explanation*'.

[9] 'ISDHESCSR"

[10] "One can only be successful if a blind location is secured where the ducks are going to fly by." *Hunting Ducks and Geese on California's Public Areas* by Richard Fletcher, Towhee Publishing, 1987. (Fletcher is loaded with great advice.)

3. "There *were* ducks where we were, but we still didn't get any."[11]

The above excuses are best summarized as follows:

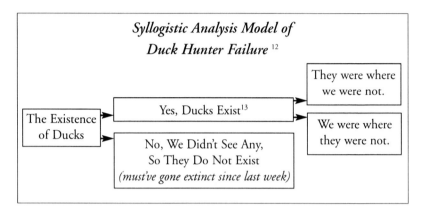

*Syllogistic Analysis Model of
Duck Hunter Failure* [12]

The Existence of Ducks	Yes, Ducks Exist[13]	They were where we were not.
	No, We Didn't See Any, So They Do Not Exist (*must've gone extinct since last week*)	We were where they were not.

Notwithstanding the simple elegance of the above rationalizations, they are not always easily put into practice. You see, duck hunting, in its own peculiar way, is too much *like life itself,* requiring that one spurn the advancement of simple, honest mitigating confessions. Lame, puerile excuses (i.e., the *truth*) impede man's—and duck hunters'—three most fundamental human instincts:

☑ *to say a lot more than he should;*
☑ *to say a lot more than others ever care to hear;*
☑ *to absolutely deny personal responsibility for one's failure.*

---

[11] Since 1983, Dorchester County, Maryland has released three million pen-raised mallards to augment diminishing wild populations . . . a dangerous precedent. Taken to its logical conclusion, this could result in hunters actually killing a limit of ducks. This in turn would stifle or eliminate the development of rich, innovative excuses for failure. Avid hunters, relishing creative excuses for failure, should act aggressively to thwart such release programs.

[12] More good advice from Fletcher: "No matter how scientific your approach, nothing will guarantee that ducks will be at any given place at any particular time." Fletcher, p.18.

[13] "If you spot ducks working a pond, that is the best evidence that you can get. If you find a spot that the ducks like, go back to it." Fletcher p. 23.

Interestingly, post-hunt chronicles are consistent nationwide, similarly expressed by bankers, farmers, plumbers and bakers from Maine to Texas, across the prairie, to California[14]: "There just weren't any ducks." This attempt at vindication is, in a word, feeble. It demonstrates the dispassionate, uncaring duck hunter, unwilling to prevaricate[15] for the good of the sport and, indeed, mankind.

I have actually discovered 4,618 discretely different 'explanations' for a bad duck hunt. However, given the constraints imposed by my fascist publisher, we reduced the number to 101.

ISDHESCSR also has identified alternative ways of categorizing excuses. This work was to better understand—therefore expand and embellish—the scope of excuses for failure available to the average duck hunter.

For example, another convenient way of considering excuses is to separate them into three categories:

1. *Acts of Nature*
2. *Acts of Man*
3. *Equipment and stuff either malfunctioning or altogether absent* [16,17]

1. Acts of Nature are the most plausible and convincing explanations. What wife or friend can argue with the capricious whims of nature?

---

[14] Californians kill more ducks than the hunters in any other state, or 1.4 million birds. Arkansas is second with 1.1 million. Arkansas leads California in numbers of mallards killed. Arkansans kill around 560,000 mallards per year, while California's take is about 360,000.

[15] In the South, synonymous with "telling tales". In the North, it's called "lying."

[16] "Without proper equipment, the hunter will fail before reaching the pond." Fletcher, p. 34.

[17] "There is not a more gadget-oriented segment of the sporting populace than waterfowlers. No duck hunter is satisfied unless he has at least two of everything and a backup in case something goes wrong with the pair he has, one of which he never uses anyhow." *Hunting Ducks and Geese*, by Steve Smith, Stackpole Books, 1984. p. 96.

The unsuccessful hunter cannot be blamed for the presence, amount, or intensity of rain, clouds, sun, wind. And for the bold excuse-maker: tsunami, cyclone, global warming, earthquake, blizzard, monsoon, or tornado. This stuff can come from anywhere . . . any time. Hey, it could happen.

2. Generally speaking, *Acts of Man* are decidedly less plausible than *Acts of Nature.* But, if there is no convenient monsoon, what's a duck hunter going to do?

The shortcomings of man are pretty conveniently further divided into three distinct categories:

a. you

b. your hunting buddies; and

c. everyone else in the world.[18]

In terms of priority-of-blame, of course, one first assigns blame for a bad hunt to strangers, interlopers, and illegal aliens. This is entirely consistent with the ancient "Law of Deflection of Personal Responsibility".

What's best is a broad-based condemnation such as, "You wouldn't have believed these guys: out of the blind every minute; constantly moving decoys around; calling like a bunch of wounded albatrosses; working a half-dozen robo ducks; sky-busting; and dressed in aluminum foil, hunter orange, and wearing mirrors. No wonder we didn't get any ducks!"

Next, if there are no unrelated third parties to be blamed, the unsuccessful hunter immediately reverts to hunting 'buddies'. "As always, Pete 'brought this', or 'didn't bring' that." It doesn't make much difference what Pete brought or failed to bring, it's the basic message that matters, i.e. it's Pete's fault.

---

[18] Wives and girlfriends, of course, have their own sub-category, but that's a different book.

"Darned Snow Geese!"

In his quest for a good excuse, the most desperate hunter will eventually revert to, heaven forbid, *himself* as the cause of an unsuccessful hunt. This is considered appropriate only when no other factor can possibly be blamed.

3. Finally, when no tsunami and no human being, including oneself, can be blamed, duck hunter may fall back on the extensive realm of equipment and devices, e.g. gun jammed; the blind fell into the water; coffee mug leaked; motor failed; truck rolled into the slough when the emergency brake 'failed'.

Dogs are a special category. They are, of course, not human, but I am loathe to assign them to the area of *Equipment and Accessories.* Some of my hunting buddies figure that dogs should be assigned to the category 'acts of nature'; others maintain there's nothing natural about retrievers at all.

Despite the blind loyalty—sometimes misplaced—and inescapably pleasing nature of our canine cousins, one must occasionally blame the 'damned dog', e.g: "Jake brought the wrong shells."; "Jake flooded the engine."; "Jake brought the Wood Duck decoys, instead of the Mallards."; "Jake forgot to change the oil in the truck." When using your dog as a reason for striking out, the best advice is the simplest: stay calm, and be sure to ignore the rolling eyes or guffaws from your audience . . . or the dog himself.

There are, of course, a number of valid excuses which fail to fall cleanly into any category. A perfect example is 'Decoy Arrangement'![19] Is this an Act of Nature, an Act of Man, or

---

[19] "Sometimes a variety of methods must be tried until something works. Other times a setup is acceptable, but the timing isn't right. Sometimes nothing will work. It's these days that provide the ultimate challenge, because duck hunting is an art. One never knows when the influences on the ducks will change, making them once again vulnerable. The many factors which influence duck behavior create a dynamic situation." Fletcher, p. 34.

Equipment Failure? Decoy Arrangement is subjective. Where one man considers the decoys perfect, another cannot help himself . . . wading or motoring back out to move a hen mallard four inches to the left.[20] And no one's even seen a duck in a week. And it's the middle of June. To one hunter, decoy arrangement is a great explanation for a failed hunt, while another less creative hunter might unimaginatively revert to 'there weren't any ducks.'

The simplest yet most profound reason for a failed hunt is a shortage of ducks. This sounds naïve, even stupid, in its simplicity. But, a shortage or ducks is an ancient and profound excuse. Edward Janes writes, "the ranks of wildfowl plummeted from 150 million to 30 million in 1934. A pathetic remnant took to the age-old flyways in that autumn of destiny, winging south over a ravaged land. The good old days were gone forever."[21]

And thousands of years before Janes' comment, the Anazazis carved petroglyphs into the rock walls of the American southwest. Renowned glyph scientists translated a scrap of Anazazi wall writing as, "I'm sorry darling, there just weren't any ducks. Guess it's salad again tonight. Back at six. Love, Og."

Generally, the serious hunter shouldn't revert to the "there weren't no ducks" excuse. Despite its grammatical redundancy . . . and accuracy . . . this unembellished explanation is the most fundamental and comprehensive account of a luckless outing. However, it is also the most crude and uninspired. Its very lack of narrative guile is reprehensible to every duck hunting enthusiast!

A note on sex, well, rather, 'gender.' (but the word sex gets your attention, doesn't it?) The use of "he" and "him" is a matter of

---

[20] There is much myth and misunderstanding regarding the duck hunting term 'stool'. Jim Low writes in The Missouri Conservationist, 'To a novice, one decoy spread looks pretty much like another. But designing a "stool" that pulls ducks in is an art.'

[21] Do not be misled. You do not have to be this lyrical . . . as you will discover as you read further.

convenience and, given that most duck hunters are male, it should not give offense. We know dames and chicks who are excellent duck hunters, and hope they will forgive our propensity to use the male gender.

As to the abundant footnotes: first, I like what other writers say. Plus, they often say stuff in a way that is more profound and accurate. Also, I want to give the interested reader some additional insights, information and background. You can just read the main text, of course, but you do that *only at risk of missing the hidden clues to the puzzle . . . with a prize of one million dollars!* [22] So, lest one suffer for lack of uninspired justifications for failure, we offer *101 Reasons for a Bad Duck Hunt:* the quintessential guide to "explanations".

(And, hint, hint, these *explanations* also work pretty damned well as excuses.) [23]

A Word on Hunters and States

Some notes on where ducks and duck hunters are found:

It makes sense that the best excuses should come out of those areas with the most duck hunters and, it would seem the fewest ducks, ergo, the least success. However, the most intensively hunted states must almost necessarily have the most ducks, else why would good citizens continue to go afield? To provide material for this book? I think not.

The most duck hunters are in Minnesota (88,000); Texas (72);

---

[22] Of course, there is no such prize. But we got you to read a footnote.

[23] "Eight times I was shutout that season. Shutouts are common in duck hunting. Four times I didn't fire a shot. On most shutouts, I had a few good chances. In six cases, I stayed and hunted until the end of shooting time, so it's not as if I didn't put forth the necessary effort." Fletcher, p.65.

Arkansas (70); Louisiana (57); Wisconsin (68); California (48); Michigan (47); and Illinois (35) . . . all in the Mississippi Flyway, except Texas (Central) and California (Pacific). In fact, the Mississippi flyway accounts for 40% to 50% of the total ducks killed in the U.S. each year. Just 7 states have one-half million licensed duck hunters!

As one might expect, there's a close relationship between the number of hunters in a state and the number of ducks harvested. Californians kill more ducks than any other state (about 1.25 million), followed by Arkansas, Louisiana, Texas, Minnesota, North Dakota, Wisconsin, Missouri, and Illinois.

Which state has the worst hunters, therefore those who need this book the most? In states with lots of ducks, one naturally expects a lot of hunters who, noticing a duck on every street corner, rush to get their shotguns. On the other hand, in states with fewer ducks, but lots of die-hard duck hunters, there might be a large number of ducks killed just because of the number of hunters in the field and their dedication. Got it?

California duck hunters kill nearly 25 per hunter. Several other states are no slouches: Louisiana (18); Delaware, Mississippi and Oklahoma (16); Utah, Delaware and Arkansas (15); with Kentucky, Mississippi, Kansas, Kentucky, Oregon, and North Dakota following (each around 14.5).

88,000 duck hunters in Minnesota, a state with around 5 million folks, is staggering. Minnesotans kill three-quarters of a million ducks each year. One out of every 58 Minnesotans is a duck hunter, or at least buys a duck stamp. (These are people that sit over man-made holes in the ice, hour by hour).

So, Californians shoot over 1.2 million ducks annually and Texans kill over 800 thousand. But those are big states: While one of every 58 persons in Minnesota is a duck hunter, in California it's one out of 770 and in Texas it's one out of 320.[24]

But the real hero is Arkansas, with one duck hunter for every 40 citizens. Even Louisiana, with 4.5 million population and nearly 60,000 duck hunters has a ratio of only one hunter per 79 people.

As far as duck hunting failure goes, the winners are Georgia, New Hampshire, Pennsylvania, Maine, and West Virginia. Annually, Pennsylvanians kill a paltry 5 ducks per hunter. In the fall, they are hunting deer, mining coal, and watching Joe Paterno coach football, pursuits at which they excel. But, Pennsylvanians are lousy duck hunters.

West Virginia' has a measly 5.2 ducks per hunter, with Maine at 5.3, New Hampshire at 5.5 and Georgia at 6.2.

So, exercising excuses for a poor hunt, best avoid Arkansas—where there are lots of ducks, lots of duck hunters, and where the duck hunters are diligent and accurate . . . or California, where hunters do pretty well.[25] To get good excuses, move on to West Virginia or Pennsylvania; though in the former there are only 1,000 duck hunters in the state and it's pretty hilly, so good luck at finding someone who hunts ducks.

---

[24] In fairness, Texans are out shooting lots of other stuff, too. After all, where else can you bag Niglai, Aoudad, Javelina, Mouflon, Jaguarundi, and Green Jay in the same day?

[25] This profound analysis ignores a major variable, i.e. time spent at the activity. Arkansas, Mississippi and California hunters spend 30 days out duck hunting every season, and West Virginians and Mainiacs hunt for an hour and ten minutes per hunter. The numbers are hardly comparable.

THE EXCUSES

Temperature

Temperature[1] *offers myriad excuses for striking out. The most important point is that the temperature—whatever it is—is never right.*

Version #1: Not Cold Enough[2]

"Well, that's right . . . just aren't no birds. They're still up in Canada (pick one: Manitoba. . . Alberta. . . Saschetwan. . . British Columbia. . . or just hanging around the CN Tower, eh?) It's just not cold enough to drive 'em down here. We need some *weather* before we can get any ducks."

Version #2: Too Cold[3]

"The birds are gone. Didn't I say so? They were here, but they're gone alright. Just too cold . . . the birds are all in Louisiana (or pick one: Port Arthur, Hobe Sound, Cozumel, La Jolla, Ixtapa).

---

[1] "The finest weather for duck shooting is what is usually denominated foul weather—windy, cloudy, rainy, often with snow squalls and a temperature so low that ice falls—the gunner must always go prepared to suffer some discomfort." Grinnell, p. 241.

[2] "Rainfall patterns are not predictable, and cold weather up north is necessary to drive the birds down to the southern sections of the flyways. The worst combination is a warm, dry year." Smith, p. 36.

[3] Grinnell, p. 241.

"Maybe it is a little cold..."

"No self-respecting mallard (or widgeon, pintail, teal; pick one) would hang around here when it's all froze up like this. We spent the entire morning breaking ice, trying to make a little hole for them.

"Plus, there's nothing to eat. If you were a mallard, it was freezing cold, and there was nothing to eat, what would you do? You'd sure go to Louisiana, right? That's right, *even* Louisiana.

"I got one shot this morning. A brace wheeled through the decoys, one of 'em wearing a Mossy Oak™ Polartec vest, and the other Cabela's Mossy Oak™ 'clava. Now, man, *that's* cold.

"Know what? My gun jammed from the cold.[4] I just don't know about that old pump, but every time it gets under thirty-below, it starts to act up."

Version #3: Hot and Calm

"We got nothing. Too hot, too calm. Worst opening weekend ever, since I started shooting chipmunks with a .410. We always pull our limits with no problem on opener . . . just way too hot and no wind.[5]

"You can shoot on a hot day, if you've got plenty of wind. And you can shoot fine with no wind, but it's got to be cold. Hot and calm don't mix when you're shooting ducks.

Author's Note: *The following should help organize your weather excuses. Only cold windy days generate excuse difficulty. On such days, one has to fall back on something simple like "It was too cold and windy for duck hunting." Be careful of your audience, lest it contain veteran duck hunters who may tell you how full of "it" you are.*

---

[4] A malfunctioning fire piece—even due to cold weather—can reasonably be assigned to "Equipment Failure".

[5] Note the casual reference to two conditions, temperature and wind, giving the excuse more force.

Analytical Model for Meteorological Excuses

Hot and windy = Poor!

Hot and calm = Forget it!

Cold and calm = No luck!

Cold and windy [6,7] = Maybe?

Version #4: Blue Bird Day

"It was a blue bird day, that's all. Simple: a blue bird day."

Version #5: Ice[8,9]

"I've never seen it frozen up like this. Six inches thick. We busted a hole in the ice and put out some decoys, but the ice kept floating back in, and the hole kept freezing over, again and again. What a mess. There were plenty of ducks in the sky, but we never fired our guns."

---

[6] Requires great creativity and imagination to explain failure.

[7] "Most often it's the weather that creates the type of day when no ducks will be killed. On six of the eight days I was "skunked", the weather was clear and ducks could be seen in all directions. Clear weather doesn't guarantee failure, but reduces the chance for success, especially if there is no wind or cold. When the weather is clear, ducks spot large concentrations of birds in safe areas, not coming down until they are over the safe area." Fletcher, p. 67

[8] "A couple of teal and goldeneye provided chances, but there was no way the dog would retrieve through the ice covered water, so the ducks were granted a reprieve." Fletcher, p. 61 (This also qualifies as a "dog excuse".)

[9] "If it be true, that enjoyment in any sport is proportioned to its difficulties and hardships, then we may readily comprehend why wildfowl shooting is popular." Grinnell, p. 241.

"You think maybe it's too hot?"

"I told you so, they're all still up north."

Location and Habits

Immerse yourself deeply enough in duck hunting research—pouring through books, pamphlets, journals and magazines—and you'll eventually notice a familiar theme: authors encourage you to go to where ducks are. Really. Thus, ducks' location—and the habits that drive them to a certain location—are paramount. Caveat: if you go where the ducks are, it severely limits your excuse-making capabilities.

Version #1: They're in the Fields

"Naw, we didn't get anything. They just won't work the timber when it's like this. They're out in the fields feeding . . . no need to come into the timber today. I *told* Kenny we should've set up in the field."

Version #2: They Fed Last Night[1,2]

"Birds fed last night . . . out in the fields feeding all night, and now they're finished feeding, just sitting somewhere. They split

---

[1] A variation relates to clear, moonlit nights, cursed by hunters. A bright moon on a cloudless night permits ducks to move around and feed during the night. "After a moonlit night, the hunting's always lousy here," one hunter said. "Where do they go?" I asked. "They don't *go* anywhere, they stay where they're at," he replied.

[2] "Overcast skies prevent ducks from feeding at night because of reduced visibility, so they feed more actively during daylight hours." Smith, p. 57

Well, the guy at that country store back
there told me that they'd be in the fields
today . . . not in the timber.

before dawn. Nobody's going to do good, if the birds already fed at night."

Version #3: Ducks in the Refuge

"They were just sittin' all day at the refuge. That's two thousand acres of open water. The ducks just go there and sit. DNR[3] has turned it into a roosting area . . . a place of peace and contentment . . . for *ducks*, that is."

Version #4: Too Many Old Birds[4]

"Too many old birds.[5] We're seeing last years' birds, all of them. They're just too smart. They've seen this before . . . just won't come on in like young birds."

Version #5: They're in the Timber[6]

"They won't work the fields, when it's like this. They're in the timber resting . . . no need to come into the fields today. We should've set up in the timber."

---

[3] Department of Natural Resources.

[4] "As the season progresses, those natives that aren't shot become damn well educated. At this time, and before the migration brings in fresh birds, the shooting gets a little slim." Smith, p. 21.

[5] After breeding season, ducks moult (shed old feathers) going into 'eclipse plumage.' Males moult first. Moms guard ducklings closely for about eight weeks, until ducklings' flight feathers appear, then leave them to feed and learn to fly. In some species, the young fly to open lakes to join the males. Females arrive later, after their moult is complete. Adult birds leave the nesting ground first, with young birds following, so early season hunting is disproportionately older birds.

[6] "Wildfowl shooting in the timber is practiced in the South when rivers overflow their banks and spread over low wooded country. When the Mississippi River breaks out of banks in the autumn and covers much of the low country, great sport may be had in the overflowed lands, to which all the fresh-water ducks resort; though most are mallards." Grinnell, p. 332.

Version #6: Ducks Holding

"We didn't get a shot. Ducks were holding. It's the same everywhere. Unfrozen lakes, ponds, and streams over all over the upper flyways . . . unseasonably warm, that's what it is. *They*[7] say there's still seven million ducks up there . . . in Wisconsin, the Dakotas, Minnesota . . . just holding. Ducks and geese are stubborn. And it's just the same in the other flyways . . . the Pacific, Atlantic, Central, and Mississippi. We're gonna strike out as long as the ducks are holding."

Version #7: Ducks Too Damned Smart

"Ducks have a very high I.Q. They don't go to college, of course. Theirs is a different kind of smarts . . . natural smarts. Here comes a dozen ducks, sailing across in front, just out of range. They take a good look, and they *know*. They are *really* smart. So there they go, they fly about two-hundred yards up, then circle down over the refuge, and drop out of the sky, like they're lead. They're educated all right."

Version #8: Feeding 'Over There'

"No ducks . . . again. Those guys across the way are feeding again. They must have bought all the corn in Nebraska! The ducks are in there day and night. I tell you, it's like cocaine or Bud Light . . . the ducks just can't resist that kind of baiting. We seen them drop in over there . . . like a magnet sucking 'em out of the sky. The shooting over there stops about seven, then they're limited out. And the ducks just

---

[7] Note the frequent use of "they", as a source. When creating excuses, "they" is *always* appropriate. It presumes to refer to some expert, a wildlife biologist, ranger, game warden, Cornell ornithology professor, or seventeen year old summer intern at the Department of the Interior. Caution: it is grossly impolite to ask another hunter, "Just who the hell is 'they' anyhow?"

"Maybe they <u>can</u> read..."

"Alright Kids, That's a blind over there...
those are hunters, and floating there in
the water are what are called Decoys."

stay all day, like it was some white table cloth restaurant or something: Chez Cracked Corn. It's illegal to hunt like that . . . somebody's going to call the wardens on those guys. Anyway, you just can't compete with corn, no way. I know for sure, because last year those guys didn't have any ducks when *we* were feeding like that."

Version #9: Ducks have 'Caught On'

While still problematic, studies at The Institute for the Measurement, Examination, and Evaluation of Duck Intelligence (IMEEDI)[8] indicate that certain species of ducks show remarkable ability to discern between certain types of decoys, old friends and families, colors and shapes, and types of sauces, particularly l'orange and cranberry.

Breakthrough research shows that those ducks fooled by robo ducks and, hence, shot and killed, are statistically less likely to pass on their respective genetic makeup to successive generations. While research is still underway, it appears that ducks that are *not* fooled by hunters are less likely to become victims of the hunter. Therefore, a higher percentage of those ducks that are *not killed* will survive over the long term. Again, got it?

Most evidence that ducks can "catch on", e.g. to 'robo ducks', is, unfortunately, anecdotal. IMEEDI, through major grants (up to $1,638.93) from the *Foundation for Avian Psychometrics, Cognition, Intelligence, and Verbal, Mathematical, Spatial, Memory and Reasoning*[9], is on the threshold of proving that many ducks do

---

[8] IMEEDI, headquartered on Maryland's Eastern Shore, has branches throughout the U.S, including Cairo, Illinois; Stuttgart, Arkansas; and Benicia, California. For a small fee, duck hunters (registrants much present a valid hunting license and current duck stamp) may take seminars on intelligence and perception abilities of wildfowl. Examples include "White Fronted versus Speckled Belly: Who Can Best Identify the Cabela Magnum Decoy" and "Smart or Lucky: Surviving Widgeons and the Stanford-Binet Test for Ducks."

[9] More commonly referred to as just *'FAPCIVMSMR'*.

indeed "catch on' to hunters' tricky devices, subsequently engaging in what IMEEDI scientists call 'Avoidance Behavior'.[10] Tests indicate that ducks failing to employ 'avoidance behavior' incur increased rates of what scientists term 'Death Behavior'.

Version #10: Flyways[11]

Essential point: of the four major flyways, the three where the hunter is *not* located (anywhere where you aren't) are loaded with ducks.

Note: because of geography, hunting pressure, breeding success, water availability, government regulations, sunspots, tides, astrological phenomena, and combinations of curses and spells invoked by witches and warlocks in other flyways, one's own flyway always suffers lower hunting success than other flyways.

Attributing failure to broad and nebulous "flyway issues" can work great with neophytes and may work well with experienced hunters, i.e. "I'll tell you what, the flyways are really messed up this year . . . birds are moving differently. Our flyway just got the brunt of it.," Stevie says.

"Really, I didn't know that," I reply.

"You didn't!" (Stevie shouts with a subtle combination of shock, consternation, and derision.) "I thought *everybody* knew what was

---

[10] A technical scientific term for ducks staying away from stuff.

[11] 'Flyway' describes a route that ducks (and many other types of birds) use to migrate in southerly and northerly directions. (After all, they have to get *back.*) Flyways conceptually represent major concentrations through 'channels' or 'funnels' of migrating birds. The Pacific represents areas west of the Rockies. The Central is through the Great Plains states; Mississippi along areas dominated by the Mississippi River, including areas east of the River forming parts of that river's basin. The Eastern represents areas east of the Appalachians. Generations of ducks tend to use the same flyways. Those breeding in specific parts of the northern U.S. and Canada (sensibly, it seems) use the most geographically proximate flyway to their breeding or wintering grounds.

happening in the flyways this year." (i.e. "You illiterate son of a retarded retriever, don't you know *squat!*")

In addition to amorphous blaming of other flyways, one may fall back on the *Season Length Axiom*, that is, other flyways get longer seasons and more hunting days than your flyway. For example, here's an excerpt from an actual explanation of season length limitations. In this case, one wants to hunt in the Atlantic Flyway, thus having the built-in excuse of the fewest hunting days available:

> *"Under the Service's late-season frameworks proposal, season lengths are 107 days in the Pacific Flyway, 74 days in the Central Flyway, 22 days in the Mississippi Flyway and 9 hours in the Atlantic. However, seasons for pintails and canvasbacks are 12 hours in the Atlantic Flyway, 39 days in the Central Flyway, 30 days in the Mississippi and Pacific Flyways. Finally, recently enacted regulation will limit whatever flyway Stevie is hunting in to twenty-eight minutes."*

Version #11: Migratory Patterns

"Migratory patterns change over time; we've done it, you know. We've forced ducks to change their migrations in such a short time. Birds go where they find food, water and safety, and they stay as long as the local habitat can satisfy those needs. You know what most hunters don't know? A duck can store up to seven days' of fat before it has to eat.[12] That's right. Mankind can change a migration. We've managed to do it. Just look at the echidna and

---

[12] Jimmie Rae's wife hunts with us sometimes. He says she could go a lot longer than seven days . . . maybe a month or two. He's never said it to her, though.

the hyrax[13], huh? Changed migratory patterns—that's why there's no ducks."

The Institute for the and Study of Duck Hunters' Experiencing Cognitive Separation from Reality secured grant monies to study ducks' presumably inherent drive for satisfying the needs of *food, water and safety.* This effort will add much to the science of understanding ducks and duck hunters.

Much of the research is based on the seminal work performed by Abraham Maslow on "Hierarchy of Needs" proposed in his 1943 paper *A Theory of Human Motivation.* Maslow[14] maintained that, as humans meet 'basic needs,' they seek to satisfy successively 'higher needs' that constitute a set hierarchy.

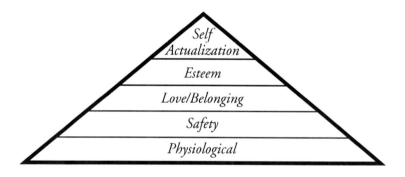

Maslow's Hierarchy of Human Needs

---

[13] The author has no idea what an echidna or a hyrax is. Jimmie Rae is usually lucid, so we accept his analogy. We know he doesn't read and all he watches is Court TV, Sponge Bob and the late Australian guy with the funny accent and khaki shorts who was always messing around with poisonous snakes and crocodiles. So the echidna and hyrax things are probably Australian.

[14] It is not known if Maslow was a duck hunter; and, whether or not he performed psychological studies on ducks. He should have, though.

Maslow's *Hierarchy of Needs* is often depicted as a five-level pyramid: four lower levels grouped as *deficiency needs* associated with physiological needs, while the top level is termed *personal growth needs* or self-actualization. Higher level needs only come into focus once all lower needs are satisfied. Simply put, a person doesn't think about the state of the universe or self-actualization when he needs a meal and a warm place to sleep. Growth forces create upward movement in the hierarchy. Regressive forces push needs further down the hierarchy.

We've discovered a Hierarchy of Needs for ducks. Duck hunters can easily comprehend a mallard's need for food, water and safety. To date, research shows that close behind food, water and safety comes the need for female accompaniment. But what if all these basic "needs" are fulfilled? When does the duck evolve (or perhaps transcend) into fulfilling even higher needs . . . his self-awareness, sense of being, need to understand his place in the higher scheme of life, enlightenment and self-actualization . . . his very "duckness"?

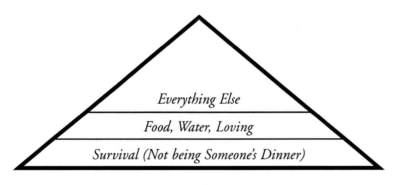

"Maslow's" Hierarchy of Duck Needs

The Institute hopes to answer these vital questions, to delve further into the mind of the duck, and eventually create new tools

"I think they're fighting back..."

enabling duck hunters to achieve success—every time out—
no excuses.

Version #12: Iowa Is Covered Up With Ducks

"They're all in (pick one: Iowa, Nebraska, British Virgin
Islands, Mall of America). That's why we can't kill any ducks.
People can make up any excuse they want and point fingers but,
truth is, the real problem is mild winters caused by El Niño, La
Niña or whatever Spanish-named affliction we are suffering at the
moment. With a really cold winter last year, with lots of snow and
ice north, we'd have *gotten* ducks and we'd have *kept* ducks."

"I know their numbers are down. I have a lot of friends who
didn't hunt near as much as they usually do. This was our second
straight mild winter and second straight horrible season. It's only
natural for people to get tired of getting up at daylight, trudging
through the muck and mud, sweating and swatting[15], just to get to
a hunting spot with no ducks.

"Last year, everyone was done by the first of January. I kept
going, and let me tell you, those guys who quit were right. The
ducks didn't come back in enough numbers to make up for all the
time and expense. But in Iowa, they're covered up with ducks."

Version #13:
They're Resting—Specific Geographic Area[16,17]

"Those birds are resting in eastern Colorado, down Highway
385 at Bonny Reservoir, north of Burlington. They're on the
sanctuary . . . millions upon millions. There's a good mix of

---

[15] Early in the season, swatting at mosquitoes. Later on in the season, at one's hunting partner.

[16] Insert geographic area of your choice, preferably with supporting detail.

[17] "There are days when ducks will not fly as they will on other days, though they still throng both lake and slough in myriads." Grinnell, p. 370.

Canadas and snows feeding in surrounding fields, but you have to ambush 'em by running out of the reeds and jump shooting them on the edge of the lake. That's not duck hunting to me. Plus, it's a lot of work."

"The rest of the ducks are in the southeast . . . so many big bodies of water . . . stretching from Queens-Neenosha to John Martin, and with plenty of places between that aren't hunted. And Queens-Neeosha lakes are protected. They're supposed to plant grain around there, but I haven't heard of any. And this even—odd number thing isn't working either."

"Birds just go rest. And we strike out."

Version #14: They're Resting—In the Refuge

"If ducks leave these refuges, there's nowhere they don't get shot at. It doesn't take a smart duck very long to figure that out. People want state officials to push waterfowl off refuges, but if and when they do, they're gone entirely. There aren't any ducks now, but if they allow hunting in the refuges, the ducks will just up and move to another refuge, or head out completely."

Version #15: Up And Left

"Leaving is exactly what ducks did last year. The state wildlife guys counted fifty thousand mallards in one area of the north Delta in the second week of December. By the fourth week, folks in that area complained there's no ducks. 'Up and left,' said one guy near Cleveland. 'We had a lot of ducks come in with one or two cold fronts, second week in December . . . stayed about a week. We hunted for about two days, without any luck, and were really excited about the next weekend. When we showed up at daylight the next week, there wasn't a duck of any kind to be found.'

"When I got home, I got on the Internet and went to the

"For gosh shakes, Ethel . . .
Don't say anything, just bobble!"

www.duck-weather.com to see what conditions were up north. Heck, it was as warm in North Dakota. Those ducks went back north. I know they didn't go back to Arkansas or over to Louisiana like a lot of people think. I've talked to friends who hunt from north Arkansas to the Gulf, and they didn't have any ducks either. Those ducks went north and didn't come back until February, when the season closed. That's right, *they just up and left.*"

Version # 16: Behavioral Change[18]

This is a great 'explanation' because it allows the amateur to engage in long discourse, sounding like he is actually knowledgeable about bioinformatics, evolutionary biology, or ornithological ecology . . . when, in reality, he hasn't got a clue. Plus, admit it, there's a little scientist in all of us and most of us can't resist the opportunity to display our expertise. Example:

"Guys at the State insist behavior has changed. They say hunting pressure is the culprit for *behavioral changes* in ducks wintering in (your state). Yup, it's *scientifically documented*: behavioral patterns are changing."

Actual words from a State Game Official explain:

"Remember, if we move birds off the refuge they are not going to a nearby sanctuary. They are going to have a bad experience and leave the area entirely."

(By "bad experience", the official presumably means that the ducks will fly into a group of fake plastic ducks and get shot by adult men with big guns.)

One state official offered a similar explanation, "Moving ducks off refuges won't work because they go to areas that are hunted.

---

[18] 'Duck Behavior' is one of the most recent excuses to evolve. It should be employed with great care.

How long would that last? Would it be one day or two, before they are back on the refuge, or worse—gone altogether? This is going to create a *permanent behavioral change*, and we surely don't want that.'

The dilemma was supposedly documented in August 2003, "Improving the Quality of Duck Hunting: Findings and Recommendations of the Arkansas Wildlife Federation Duck Committee." This lengthy title boils down to 'behavioral change' and permanently changing the habits of ducks:

> *Workable / huntable ducks, those that come to a call or decoy spread[19], are not the norm anymore. Among the behavioral changes are ducks that cling to refuges throughout the season and seldom wander off to provide hunting opportunity. And in some cases, when birds venture onto private or public hunting grounds—it is only to feed at night. One great way to improve duck hunting is to decrease the number of legal hunting days or shorten legal hunting hours.[20] If bad duck hunting were happening in one specific area, it might be okay, but we don't have any working[21] ducks . . .the problem of unsuccessful duck hunting is widespread. No doubt we have altered duck behavior in recent years.*

"One slow morning, Cappie speculated that it wasn't that the birds were actually *learning* to avoid us, rather, it was that they *didn't have to learn.*

"Cappie says 'all they got to do is have a bunch of 'em die for the cause.' When we inquired as to what in the be-jesus he meant,

---

[19] i.e. stupid ducks.

[20] The "hunt less, and your hunting will improve" logic to which some conservation officials descend, not unlike road signs saying, 'This lane closed for your convenience'. Or, 'Your call is very important to us . . . the wait for a customer service representative is thirty-three minutes.'

[21] "Working ducks" is a euphemism for "stupid ducks". The expression "working" ducks has nothing to do with ducks actually holding down jobs.

"Brant, Canada, Specks...Nope no mention
of Mother Goose."

Cappie says that 'the dumb ones die and the smart ones live. Then the only babies are babies of smart ones . . . except some dumb baby ducks hatch out anyway. But next season, the ducks are all a little smarter, *maybe just incrementally so*', Cappie stressed. When Cappie starts using expressions like *'incrementally so'*, it's time to pick up the decoys and go watch some football. Cappie goes on, 'In time, there will be no duck hunting at all, because as ducks get smarter and smarter—by virtue of us killing all the stupid ones—all ducks will be brilliant. At that point they'll not only avoid us completely, but they'll start inventing stuff and reading books.'

"Kevin, who has a load of degrees and shoots with a skill level inverse to his education, jumped in to clarify. 'Cappie means there is a natural process ordaining that individual organisms endowed with favorable traits—in this case, ducks being able to spot Cappie's always jumping around in the blind—will reproduce at greater degrees than individuals not so endowed with favorable traits. There is a constant and continual evaluation of the performance of each individual as it seeks to survive, bearing a modestly or markedly different phenotype than other individuals of the same type. Harvard's evolutionary anthropologic paleontologist Steven Jay Gould termed this 'punctuated equilibrium', long periods of evolutionary stability broken by shorter spurts of evolutionary change, perhaps sparked by external events. In this case, the critical evaluation mechanism—the end to stability marked by an external event—is the blast of a shotgun propelling small metal pellets at the organism at rates of up to two thousand feet per second and by their force ending the existence of a duck. When a specific individual's phenotype allows that individual organism to differ, in some favorable sense, from others of its species, and that favorable trait is heritable, it flows logically that the frequency of the trait will increase over some number of generations. Thus, our very hunting is forcing the evolution of adaptive alternations in the genetic structure of the specie we hunt, thereby making each hunt marginally less successful. We have met the cause of our poor duck hunting . . . and it is *us!* We have now isolated and identified the contribution of our own efforts to adaptive organismic characteristics.'

"Louie, who had been cleaning the treads of his waders with a toothbrush (that he later used on his tooth), thought he heard the word 'orgasm' and perked up. When Louie pays any attention to anything that Cappie or Kevin has to say, it's time to go in for breakfast or lunch or whatever. And we did. Without ducks, I might add."

Version # 17: Canada[22,23]

"You know where these ducks come from, right? Canada. All of 'em comes from Canada. Yeah, these are Canadian ducks you're shooting or, in this particular case, *not* shooting.

"Why, I saw a bunch of greenheads last year and they all had red maple leafs on their chests. Proud birds, they were. Billy Joe claims he heard a bunch of 'em quackin' *O Canada* in Quebecqois! He thought for a second he was at a Leafs—Canadiens game.

"And ol' Anders Brastad, out in the county, well, he says that last year he got passed all day by mallards going, 'quack, quack, *eh?*'

"Well, I don't know about that, but I know that if it weren't for Canada, we wouldn't *have* any ducks. Saskatchewan, Manitoba, Alberta . . . those mean anything to you? You go up to Raven, north of Saskatoon, and you'll pretty quick see where those ducks get laid. Or 'hatched', if you prefer.

---

[22] "Today, we worry about droughts on the Canadian prairies, about pesticide accumulations, about farming practices that drain potholes, and about what the Corps of Engineers has up its sleeve." Smith, p. 55.

[23] "The North American waterfowl resource is primarily dependent on the prairie wetlands in Canada . . . .70 percent of ducks are produced in the Prairie Pothole Region of Canada." *Fireside Waterfowler,* edited by David E. Wesley and William G. Leitch, Ducks Unlimited, 1987.

"They went North . . . They went South . . .
Let's go home."

"So, here's ol' Canada sitting up on top of the U.S., and those Canucks are fat, dumb and happy with all the duck nesting areas belonging to them in that friendly North Country. But you think any Canadian cares about whether Billy Joe and I kill any ducks down here? No, not by a long shot they don't.

"*O Canada* we stand on guard for thee", all right! Except the 'thee' isn't us down here. The 'thee' is ducks, that's who it is. Canadian ducks. That's who they really stand on guard for!"

Version # 18: Ducks on the Big Water

"Big water. That's what it's all about. This time of year, this kind of weather, well, the ducks just want to sit all day on big water."

Version #19: Clear Night in the Timber[24]

For green timber hunters, moonlit, cloudless situations can sometimes be a paradox. The hunters want clear cloudless days, because the birds will work better into the timber when it is clear. However, clear mornings often follow clear nights, and that's when the ducks tend to feed in the timber, then in the early morning fly out to go and sit somewhere for the day.

---

[24] "If shot at night, it must be a cloudy night with a moon. On a bright moonlight night the birds cannot be seen unless they pass very near, and even then he is likely to have only a glimpse, while if a bright moon is shining behind clouds, the diffused light renders the whole sky so light ducks can be seen quite a long way off and the gunner has little difficulty knowing when and where to shoot." Grinnell, p. 332. When Grinnell wrote, it was legal to hunt at night. Today, it will get you six months behind bars.

Wind

Wind[1,2,3,4] *is an ever-present excuse for striking out on a duck hunt. It's a lot like temperature . . . what ever it is, it's wrong. Thus, you don't necessarily have to have your motor fall off the back of your boat. For the less creative, wind is always there, and it's always from the wrong direction.*

Version #1: From the South

"Plenty of birds . . . just won't work a *south* wind like this. . . you don't get 'em when the wind's comin' up out of the south like today."

Version # 2: From the West

"Plenty of birds around . . . they just won't work a *west* wind.

---

[1] "I like to use an opening—not a J rig as I would for divers—between loose groups of decoys. The intention is for the birds to come right at you in your blind and set down in the opening. To make this happen, you have to have the wind at your back." Smith, p. 24.

[2] "The hunters wrongly set up with the wind in their faces, which meant that any birds coming to the blocks would come in from behind them in order to land into the wind." Smith, page 128.

[3] "The desirable wind for point shooting is one quartering from behind the gunner. This gives the birds abundant room to swing over the water and to come up to the decoys, offering a good shot to the man in the blind." Grinnell, p. 397

[4] "Since duck hunting depends much upon the wind and its direction, some blinds are ideal for some winds and worthless for others." *The Duck Hunter's Handbook* by Bob Hinman, Winchester Press, 1974, p. 193.

"Think maybe it's too windy?"
"Naw . . . you got to have a little breeze
for good duck hunt."

It's never quite right when the wind's out of the west. They either sit tight or they just won't work right."

Version #3: From the East

"Birds won't work a *east* wind this time of year. It's never right when the wind's out of the east. The birds either sit tight or just won't work right. Birds don't like an east wind and neither do I."

Version #4: From the North

"Birds just won't work a *north* wind. Never right when the wind's out of the north. They sit tight or just won't work right. A north wind is bad."

Version #5: In Our Faces[5]

"Birds won't land with the wind. . . gotta land into the wind . . . at least quarter with it. So, we got wind in our faces, hard as hell all day. We get a couple of looks, but nothing's going to pitch with this wind. We've got no water behind us and pretty tall brush and trees behind us, too. Ducks can't come in from the back and won't land with the wind. We got skunked."

Version # 6: Changed On Us[6]

"We got our decoys set . . . took us an hour . . . as soon as we

---

[5] "Worse, the fowl can no longer swing over the water, but must swing over a marsh and come from behind the gunner and over his blind. Thus, they are certain to see him, or at least some of the strange objects he has brought into the marsh; or if they do not see him, he is obliged to twist around and shoot when they are coming toward him and nearly over his head." Grinnell, p. 397.

[6] "Sometimes, after one has tied out just right and everything favorable, the wind will haul in front of him, or may shift suddenly, blowing directly in the gunner's face. The decoys, instead of riding in a long line head to tail, swing around and now sit side by side." Grinnell, p. 397.

get back in the blind the wind changes. Now the decoys are wrong and nothing's coming in. So we gotta get back out and reset a hundred decoys. We're in the middle of the decoys and naturally birds are everywhere. So, soon as we're in the blind, the wind shifts. This goes on all morning, and we can't get it right. Guys around us are doing okay, but we never got our decoys right with the wind."

Version #7: Not Enough Wind

"You can't hunt with no wind. The birds sit tight. It takes a pretty good wind to get them moving, and look at your decoys sitting there lifeless[7] on calm, still, glassy water."

Version #8: Too Much

"You can't hunt with this much wind. The birds sit tight. They're not going to move and look at your decoys rolling unnaturally on the wind-blown water. Ducks keep on going."

---

[7] Note that decoys are 'lifeless', whether there is wind or not, because if decoys weren't lifeless, they would be living ducks, which they are not.

"Gosh, I think it's too windy."

Agriculture,
Wetlands and Habitat[1,2,3]

The loss of wetlands is an ongoing crisis, and wetland losses continue to outdistance wetland gains. The good news is that 'habitat' provides boundless excuses for failed hunting trips.

Version #1: Not Enough Farmland

"Just isn't enough farmland . . . everything's being developed. We got Starbuck's and Bed Bath and Beyond where our cornfield was. Between the strip malls and the zero lot line developments, how can you bring home ducks?"

Version #2: Loss of Bean Fields[4]

"You can't get decent money for beans. It costs more in gas, labor and equipment than you get for the beans. Large parts of this

---

[1] Every day, 12 square miles of farmland are converted to nonagricultural uses. In the 1980s, every year 1.5 million acres of cropland and open space were converted to urban and suburban use. During the 1990s, the rate doubled to 3.2 million acres per year.

[2] "The true reason for the decrease of birds is the spread of civilization, which means their destruction by civilized man; and every attempt to cover up this truth and lay blame elsewhere is a real injury to the cause of game protection." Grinnell, p. 596.

[3] "The Great Northern Plain is less than 10 percent of U.S. waterfowl breeding area, but produces 70 percent of the total duck crop." Wesley, ed. p. 31.

[4] In 1980, the spot market for soy beans reached $7.50 a bushel, with some sales in the 1990s at over $12.00. Today, beans go for about $4.50 per bushel. On an inflation-adjusted basis, beans are now around $2.50, a 70% drop from 1980.

country have got no bean fields. And, if there's no bean fields, surprise, surprise . . . there's no ducks. Why? I'll tell you why. Because a farmer can't make it on what they're paying him. Bean farmers might as well cut hay or plant pine, like everybody else.

"The international market is killing us, too. We send a couple of billion dollars down to South America to teach them how to cultivate soybeans. The friendly folks in Washington encourage us to export our know-how, technology, chemicals, pesticides, and genetic strains. It doesn't take an Andrew Einstein to guess what we're gonna get in the end. You got it. By 2020, Brazil and Argentina will be producing half of the world's beans.

"That's where we need to duck hunt: Brazil and Argentina . . . where there's ducks. The ducks go where the beans are. And that certainly isn't here, *entiendes lo que quierodecir, amigo?*"

Version #3: Loss of Ricefields

"Pretty soon, when there's no more rice, there's no more ducks.

"First you got stem borers: yellow stem borers, white stem borers, striped stem borers, dark-headed stem borers, and more. Then, there's defoliators like rice leaffolders, caseworms, leafhoppers, and *neph nigropictus, neph parvus* and *neph cincticeps.*

"The brown planthopper, rice grain bug, Malayan black rice bug, and rice field rats—mostly *Rattus rattus argentiventer* and *Rattus rattus Mearns*, for sure . . . all stealing rice from the ducks and from us!

"And what about viral disease, bacteria, fungus, and their 'vectors'? You got rice tungro, ragged stunt and *Xanthanomonas oryzae*, blast, and sheath blight.

"Add *Agertum conzoides, Fimbristylis miliacea* and—worst of all—*Monochoria vaginalis*—no, don't ask why it's called that—and it's amazing there's any rice in the whole country. And where we hunt, if there isn't good rice, there aren't ducks.

"You boys are in my rice field.
Wanna buy a nice dog?"

"Get this: the world's top rice exporting countries are Thailand, Vietnam, China and India, *followed* by the U.S. Per capita, world rice consumption is dropping. Can you imagine India and China as rice exporting countries? If we want good duck hunts, we're gonna have to speak Hindi or Mandarin."

Version #4: Delay in Rice Harvesting[5]

"You can't rely on rice farmers anymore. They're irresponsible. I told Kenny that I never met a responsible rice farmer. Kenny says that's because I never met *any* rice farmer. True, but that's not the whole story. They delayed the rice harvest again, on purpose, to confound duck hunters. Right now, there's nothing for ducks to eat."

Version #5: Fields Plowed Wrong

"Fields not being chisel plowed is making it impossible to get ducks this year."

Version #6: Loss of Wetlands[6,7,8,9]

"No decent hunting without a place for ducks to hang out. They need somewhere to breed, too. Heck, if it weren't for D.U.,

---

[5] Most effective in parts of Arkansas, California, Louisiana and Texas. Generally a weak excuse for Manitoba.

[6] The U.S. loses 100,000 wetland acres a year. Since 1800, we've lost 60% of total wetlands. Indiana, Ohio, Missouri, Iowa, Illinois, Louisiana, California and Kentucky have each lost 80% of their original wetlands. On the bright side, it provides great excuses. (Mother Nature, to little avail, keeps trying to get her wetlands back, mostly by floods and hurricanes.)

[7] "Good waterfowl areas have decreased alarmingly during the past forty-plus years. Land developments for maximum agricultural use, along with greater call for and cost of water has had major effects on California's waterfowl. California waterfowl during the past 12 years have decreased thirty percent." Fletcher, p. 85.

[8] "It is the continuing destruction of flooded woodlands that caused the biggest problems for the wood ducks' nesting needs. The draining of backwater sloughs to create more farmland hurt these ducks immensely." Smith, p. 41

we'd be out here in a burnoose, eating dates, riding over sand dunes hunting for camels."

Version #7: Bad Nesting Season[10]

"Fish 'n' Wildlife[11] says it was a bad nesting season. It's the water, pesticides or something like that. Birds just didn't nest right. Nothing you can do. Get a bad nesting season and just forget about killing birds. If it wasn't for *Ducks Unlimited*, we wouldn't have *seen* a single bird today."

Version #8: Loss of Green Timber[12]

"The logging guys come in the summer, when it's all dried out, and cut like crazy. I guess loggers have to make a living, too, but there's no decent forestry practices left. The state and private landowner, both want money. Cut, cut, cut. There's not enough green timber left to make the hunting worthwhile."

Version #9: Too Much Private Land[13]

"There's not enough public land to hunt on. The amount of state and federal refuge land is still a pittance compared to the hundreds of

[9] "As rangeland and hay meadows are converted to row crop and alfalfa production, nesting cover is destroyed and as irrigation increases, the supply of underground water is depleted, the water table falls, reducing the size and number of permanent wetlands available through the dry years." Wesley, ed. p.37.

[10] "Nebraska's rainwater basin area is no longer a production area, because of the loss of over 80 percent of the small wetlands to drainage, filling and encroachment by agriculture and development." Wesley, ed. p 37.

[11] The U.S. Fish and Wildlife Service (www.fws.gov), part of the Interior Department (www.doi.gov), as its name implies, regulates hunting and fishing. Every state has its own such department. When duck hunters refer to "the government", they usually mean FWS.

[12] "The first real concerted attack on lowland forests came from lumber companies, clearing land for virgin hardwood, then selling it for cropland.." Wesley, ed. p. 220.

[13] "With the very limited private marshlands today, the duck picture is not very bright." Ray Burmaster, California duck hunter. 2004.

millions of acres of private land, particularly agricultural land, where ducks eat. There may be ducks, but it's still tough to get to them . . . unless you have a hundred thousand bucks to join a private club."

Version #10: Too Much Public Land

"Private clubs bought up all the good marsh land and everything is posted. Between the fat cats controlling hunting land and the state buying up land and increasing refuges, it's a wonder we can even find a place anymore."

Version #11: Private Club

"The problem is private clubs. Why, when I first started hunting, you could just set up anywhere around here. Now, it's all been bought up by doctors, lawyers, dentists . . . rich guys from (pick one: Baltimore, Cairo, Helena, Opelousus.)

Version #12: Farmers[14,15,16]

"It all comes down to farmers . . . they don't give a darn about hunting, wetlands, or ducks. Just getting a government subsidy . . . that's all they care about. And making sure they farm right to the edge of every field, leaving nothing, no place for ducks to breed, hang out, have a little fun."

---

[14] Farmers are actually the last people to blame for bad duck hunting. But when you look for excuses, everybody's fair game, so to speak.

[15] "Then came the 1900s with new machinery, expanded markets and money madness that would not end until Black Tuesday in 1929. A wave of great drainage projects swept the nation. Vast marshes, hitherto inviolate where waterfowl nested and wintered for ages past, yield to new technical knowledge and the new economic order. Farmers, aided by the government, drained sloughs and marshes and changed the course of rivers to make valuable grain grow where only worthless wildfowl had resorted thereto." Janes, p. 11.

[16] "As soon as white settlers moved in, wetlands began to disappear. The fetile prairie soils produced bumper crops, and wetlands were soon drained when they proved to be a nuisance. Crops were more important than ducks." Wesley, ed. p. 31

"I could have sworn there was a marsh
here last year."

"Have a good hunt! Alright son, go turn out some more of those ducks."

Institutions

Blaming abstract organizations, associations, or a government entity is a great excuse for striking out on a hunt. Plus, it has the added advantage of not having to blame individual persons who might be able to actually defend themselves.

Version #1: Predator Management—
Not Enough Trapping[1,2,3,4]

"Up North in the pothole region, they haven't been managing the predators. Skunks, coons, foxes. . . all gone hog wild . . . so to speak. Nobody traps anymore . . . can't get a decent price for

---

[1] "As trapping becomes less profitable, the number of trappers has dropped. In Minnesota, licensed trappers plunged from 24,000 in 1980 to fewer than 5,000 in 2000. Virginia also has experienced a dramatic drop in trappers: from 5,000 in the 1970s to fewer than a thousand today." PETA Media Center, 2006.

[2] "Research provided overwhelming evidence of the serious impact of predation on nests and nesting hens. Recent studies show that removal of mammalian predators from areas of high nest density can boost nest success from 10 percent to 80 percent." The Concerned Duck Hunters Panel.

[3] "All-terrain vehicles, particularly the three-wheeler, create a means of access to formerly difficult country, making nests easy prey for foxes, gulls, and other predators." Wesley, ed. p. 51.

[4] "The principal reason for low nest success was predation. The impact of predation has increased as a consequence of man's impact on the prairie. Another major change is alternation of the composition and abundance of predator species. Settlement has benefited most present-day predators." Wesley, ed. p. 64, 65.

"I swear... I'm a duck! Just listen:
'Quack, Quack, Woof.' Oops..."

the skins. Trapper man works a fourteen-hour day and gets a couple of bucks, that's all."

Version #2: The Anti-Fur People[5]

"It's the anti-fur people, it is. People won't wear fur because they're so disruptive . . . spraying ketchup as they walk through Grand Central Station. It's not right. Nobody wears fur today, because the anti-fur folks make them feel so bad. Meanwhile, varmints are tearing up these ducks, eating the eggs and the little ones . . . poor little fluffy things. That's why the duck hunting's so poor. How am I going to get a limit with anti-fur people bringing down the duck population the way they do?"

Version #3: Power Plants

"I'll tell you hunting isn't like it was before we had these power plants up and down the river. Every power plant creates a nice little warm-water reservoir that holds thousands—maybe billions— of ducks *all winter*. They should let us shoot over the power plant discharge ponds. Most of them aren't even nuclear."

Version #4: Socialist State

"There's no such thing as socialist duck hunters, but this damned state is a socialist republic. Those bureaucrats are too busy minding other people's business and destroying the self-government we once had here in the good old U.S. of A. And those Fish & Wildlife people are commies. All they can say is 'shorter season',

---

[5] "Growth in quasi-conservation groups seriously threatens waterfowl abundance. Sportsmen have a long history of providing 'bucks for ducks' and applying pressure on politicians to protect habitat. However, every time anti-hunting groups stop a hunt, giving hunting a bad name, and discouraging hunters from actively defending their sport, wildlife's major ally weakens a bit more." Wesley, ed. p. 52.

'lower limits', 'more property for non-hunting areas.' Like we're turning into France, but without any decent brie or Beaujolais."

Version #5: Ducks Unlimited[6]

"Understand what DU's *really* up to? See, DU pays folks to plant crops. Yeah, they say they just work with landowners to improve duck habitat. Now, DU's creating habitat projects in the middle of the continent. They used to concentrate efforts on breeding grounds. But these days they're providing so-called 'habitat' throughout the Flyway, keeping birds from migrating South. Plus, DU makes warm-water wetlands so ducks stay up north all winter. Hell, they dump corn by truckloads, even by helicopter. Jimmy's seen them do it, mostly at night . . . so we won't find out."

Version #6: State Doesn't Know How to Set Bag Limits[7,8,9,10,11]

In the 1600s, a Marylander estimated one flock of ducks in the Chesapeake Bay to be a mile wide and seven miles long. By the 1800s, a Philadelphia physician and sportsman observed that "the bay shore, long before dawn of day, for miles and miles, is alive with shooters; every passing point is occupied with eager marksmen."

In 1916, the United States and Canada signed the Migratory Bird Treaty, allowing the federal government to regulate waterfowl

---

[6] Caution: Blaming DU for bad duck hunting demonstrates the perversity of otherwise mentally stable sportsmen, who have gone duckless in a couple of outings. For folks in the hunting *and* conservation fields, DU is synonymous with wetland and habitat restoration and preservation. Trigger Bob said it best when, dragging on a generic brand cigarette, he inhaled deeply holding the smoke in his no-doubt-brownish lungs, and said: "Blaming DU for hunting problems is like me blaming my pulmonologist for this emphysema thing I got."

[7] Within boundaries established by international treaties, state wildlife commissions determine season length, bag limits, and areas for migratory bird hunting.

hunting. Market hunting was banned, spring shooting outlawed, and season and daily bag limits established for hunters for the first time. The moves failed to stem the decline in waterfowl numbers.

Atlantic Flyway surveys showed duck totals fell by half, from 3 million to about 1.5 million from 1956 to 2001. The puddle duck[12] population itself fell by sixty percent over this period.

One problem with bag limits as an excuse is that duck hunters need a Ph.D. (or no education at all) to interpret them. For example, here is an exert from actual state regulations:

---

[8] "Bag Limits" is a fancy term for how many ducks you can (legally) shoot, in conjunction with stipulations on when, where, and how you can shoot them. Bag limits are based on population counts, scientific surveys showing which species has the highest breeding success, and what tastes the best. That applies except in Louisiana, where bag limits are set per the rule: 'How many can we kill before the Feds say it's too much and file an injunction . . . or we get caught?', plus interpretation of goat entrails for additional scientific support.

[9] "The Chesapeake Bay is covered with wildfowl in such abundance as are not in all the world to be equaled." William Strachey, 1610

[10] "Adaptive Harvest Management's reliance on the status of mid-continental mallards to determine annual seasons and bag limits may lead to unintentional over-harvest of other mallard populations as well as other species." Concerned Duck Hunters Panel. Duluth, Minnesota, 2002.

[11] "Present season lengths and bag limits encourage high harvests, perhaps at the expense of breeding population." Concerned Duck Hunters Panel.

[12] Puddle ducks, also called 'dabblers' are birds of fresh, shallow marshes and rivers, rather than large lakes and bays. They usually feed by dabbling or tipping, rather than submerging. Ducks feeding in croplands will be puddle ducks, being relatively sure-footed, able to walk and run well on land. Their diet is mostly vegetable, and grain-fed mallards or pintails or acorn-fattened wood ducks are highly regarded as food by many four-legged and two-legged mammals.

"I think we should keep a close eye on
the new member of the flock."

STATE OF *(Your State)*
Migratory Waterfowl Hunting Regulations

Section One (of Eighty-Three)
(Hunters must memorize all Eighty-Three Sections):

(a) For 2008, the season is in three segments, unoriginally referred to herein as Segments One, Two, and Three. Segment One shall run from November 12th through November 13th, but includes Nov 14th in the Southwest Zone only; and November 18th in the Ocean Zone for Whistling Tree Duck hens .

(b) Shooting hours are in State Fish and Game Department Regulation 143-a.1. (Check regulations for changes in shooting hours, as 'sunrise' and 'sunset' are not terms fixed by state regulation. The Department of Natural Resources, Fish and Game Division, takes no responsibility for failure of the sun to rise or set on time or, for that matter, at all.)

(c) In the North Central Zone, Segment Three commences January 19th for coots and mergansers; January 21st for Pintail; January 33rd for Canvasback and all other ducks with orange webbed feet, unless hatched in Saskatchewan.

(d) Non orange-footed ducks (regardless of webbing) born in Canada (other than Saskatchewan), are limited to one of each sex, one of each species, but not two of the same sex or species. Hunters may take more than one duck after sundown in the North Central Zone for the duration of Segment Three, except for January 25th for Pintail, January 26th for Mallards, and the morning of January 13th for Eider Duck drakes.

(e) Morning is defined for regulatory purposes as that portion of the day which is not night and which is not afternoon, regardless of the hour. Note that the state bases its time calculations upon Greenwich Median Time only in leap years.

(f) The taking of Hooded Mergansers at any time during Segment Two—in the South Central Zone or Central South Zone—is strictly prohibited, unless the hunter has purchased the special—South Central or Central South—Segment Two Hooded Merganser License.

(g) The Special South Central, Segment Two Hooded Merganser License applies only after November 15th, unless that date is a Thursday, and State's football team is ranked fifth or better in the BCS standings.

(h) Senior Citizens enjoy an extended season this year. Hunters over age eighty-eight may hunt through December 32nd in the Lake Zone during Segment One, if accompanied by a minor to whom they are not related. Seniors may also take up to three Brant before January 19th, provided they actually cook and eat them.

(i) Brant must be clearly marked with a "Brant Tag" (available for $15 at Fish and Wildlife offices throughout the State, if you can find one and it is open, or online at *www.fishandwildlife/brant/areyoureallygonnaeatoneofthose things?waittilyousmellit!.state.gov.*)

(j) Youth Hunting Season is two days only, February 4th through February 18th and applicable to mornings only, unless afternoon hunting is or becomes permissible. (Special note: "Youth Hunting" refers to youths *being the hunter.* The Department of Child Protective Services reminds adult hunters of the confusion we experienced

"Man, I don't know what's keeping the ducks away... something keeps flaring them."

last year. At *no time* may adults go hunting for youths and shoot at them during Youth Hunting Season.)

(k) Youths are defined as humans of any of the three genders legal in the state, aged six through fifteen, but not older or younger. Other hunters shall be considered 'adults'. (Child Protective Services claims this means individuals five years old and younger are defined 'adults', but we had already printed the regulations and we didn't understand their point anyway, and the governor is a duck hunter, so it'll all work out.)

(l) Hunters in Lake and Ocean Zones in the Northwest or West Central Zone may take up to a whole bunch of Gallinules, Moorhens and Coots, during Segment One, if Segment Two has not yet commenced. Taking ducks during Segment Two in Lake Zone Management Wildlife Area Southeast is strictly prohibited almost all the time.

(End of Section One)

Version #7: Helpful Hints from a State Official[13,14]

"To assist the hunter, we have reduced the bag limit and season length.

"Habitat in nesting areas was better last spring, but we just thought we'd wait to see what happened, anyway.

"As we have reported for the last eighteen consecutive years, we're probably just one harsh winter away from an excellent duck season.

---

[13] These *actual comments* from a state gaming (not casino gaming, but it might as well have been) official should provide the hunter with an excuse or two.

[14] Billy Ray says he's going to file a lawsuit against a lack of cold weather up north or rain down south. He says he knows how to do it and he's got a lawyer who'll help him for no fee, called *pro boner*. Johnny says he expects stiff opposition.

But it doesn't matter how much grain is on the ground. If deep snow covers it, birds can't eat and they move. One good snowstorm, ducks head south. That didn't happen last winter. This year we hope and pray for a massive snowstorm to absolutely cripple the north central states, and get their ducks moving down here.

"We need a wet fall and winter, too. We need water on the ground, in our sloughs, our breaks, our fields, our ponds, to hold the ducks if winter pushes them here. And, if winter doesn't push the ducks here, remember that we have excellent bowling facilities throughout the state.

"Many variables affect our season. Severe winters up north, wet weather here, duck population trends, migration routes—think about all that. It is amazing that the average duck hunter puts up with either Mother Nature or your friendly State Fish and Game Division."

Version #8: Government Working Against Us[15,16]

"The government is over-planting, even scattering grain on national refuges where hunting isn't allowed. That's the word out of Washington, anyway. They're supposed to be helping protect our constitutional right to hunt, but they're closet duck lovers, that's what. We'll never get shooting until they stop feeding over that protected land."

---

[15] Caleb says that duck hunting is specifically protected in the Bill of Rights. Jefferson and those guys knew what they were doing.

[16] "The public was suspicious not just about the Corps, but about government. The number of people who believe that 'government is run by people who don't know what they're doing' climbed from 27 percent in the early 1960s to 63 percent in 1980. In short, both a lack of confidence in government and concerns about the environment generate opposition to water projects." *Our History*, by the U.S. Army Corps of Engineers.

"Wait! Here it is! Gadwall...a medium
sized, mottled..."

Version #9: Season's Too Short[17,18]

"The season is just too short. Opened the day before yesterday and closes next week. You can't kill ducks with season dates like this."

Version # 10: Corps of Engineers[19,20]

"The Corps of Engineers has yet to see a marsh or wetland it couldn't drain or a stream or river it couldn't straighten or, in the secret code of the Corps, 'channelize'. We have a synonym for 'channelize'. . . . it's 'ruin'. They've ruined a great part of natural America and the duck habitat . . . all in the name of 'flood control'.

They can do it all: levees, water-storage areas, channel 'improvements', huge pumps, dredges, better 'drainage technology', legions of lawyers and short-sighted bureaucrats. After a couple of hundred years of Corps' 'flood control', it's amazing there's any marsh left."

Version #11: Short-Stopping

"The ducks have been short-stopped in the Midwest.

---

[17] "The basic framework for season extension was a political action, not supported by existing science." Concerned Duck Hunters Panel.

[18] "Ducks are long-lived birds. Older hens are more likely to be successful breeders. Regulations should reflect the importance of protecting breeding stock." Concerned Duck Hunters Panel.

[19] "Since the 1960s, the Corps has become more sensitive to environmental objections, changes having been forced by litigation." L.A. Times, September, 2005.

[20] "In the last 30 years, changing values, political shifts, and economic constraints have forced major alterations in the Corps' water resources program. Beginning in the 1960s, an increasingly urbanized, educated society focused more on environmental preservation, and water quality than on irrigation, navigation, or flood control. Passage of the Wilderness Act, Wild and Scenic Rivers Act, and National Environmental Policy Act testified to the strength of these new interests. The focus on the environmental consequences contributed to opposition to water projects. The Corps, the nation's largest water resources developer, received the brunt of the criticism." *Our History*, Corps of Engineers.

Intentionally, too. Folks up there have been doing it for years, and now that so many landowners are getting paid by the government through WRP and CRP, it's really brutal. No birds are coming down here."

Version #12: Bad Enforcement—Too Much

"Everywhere there's game wardens or state wildlife officials hanging around messing up the hunting. I know they have to do their job, but they don't need to scare all the ducks away, checking every blind every ten seconds, riding around in their boats chasing away all the ducks."

Version #13: Bad Enforcement—Not Enough[21]

"We *have* to have better enforcement . . . more wardens and game officials checking on hunters. Guys are taking ducks way over their limits. Some hunters shoot a limit, go back in, then come back out and shoot another limit . . . then do it all over again. The government has got to stop this."

---

[21] "Present enforcement efforts are inadequate to discourage unlawful waterfowl hunting." Concerned Duck Hunters Panel.

"Yeah, these reloads might be
a little hot."

Guns and Shooting

Dressing like weeds, lurking behind bushes, concealing oneself, peeking out of a brushy blind over a dozen plastic decoys makes little sense unless you shoot. Some device to bring the duck into your bag is indispensable, of course. This device is a shotgun.[1] Without armament, the escapade is called 'bird watching'.[2]

Version #1: Light Loads

"The problem was light loads. Stupid, not paying attention. (Too many people at my Bass Pro Shop[3].) My gun just won't eject those light loads. We get in a bunch, I get one shot off, the shell doesn't eject, and that's the only shot I got all day. Anyway, they had great prices on light loads, so I got ammo for doves and quail next year. I usually hate big-box discounters, but I walked out of Bass Pro with a new shell bag, a couple of dozen decoys, three new calls, a very nice Ducks Unlimited

---

[1] "A shotgun is the best weapon for ducks, but there is little agreement on anything else pertaining to the matter. A gun is a highly personal object, reflecting individual tastes and preferences as well as the conditions under which the individual shoots. Hinman, p 45.

[2] What duck hunters do most of the time anyway. Thus, a 'bad duck hunt' is often really a 'good bird watching excursion'.

[3] For many hunters, BPS is the "go to" place for all kinds of stuff, the only problems: a) there are so many stores—must be hundreds, b) there's too much stuff and the prices are too low. I told Sally I was going to pick up something and return in an hour. She is still furious, because I returned in four days, seventeen hours, and thirty-six minutes. I just said, "Hey, you gotta see the store before you complain."

ceiling fan, a DU cheese grater, and a neat decoy lamp. And, by the way, Sally doesn't need to know about all that stuff."

Version #2: Bad Gun[4]

"My new shotgun is a piece of duck dung. Locks up . . . jams, catches shells. I don't even want to clean the sucker . . . that would be too good for it. It's heavy, it recoils, it's the devil. That's my third busted hunt this season, trying to use that oversized paperweight."

Version #3: Steel Shot[5]

"Steel shot is the worst—and the best—thing that's happened in a long time. I've tried Kent tungsten-matrix loads, #4s and #5s, and copper coated steel B, BB, and even BBB.

"I've shot a lot of bismuth, too, money just flies right out of the end of the barrel . . . like shooting dollars, not ducks, as we say.

"Problem is, none of these are as good as lead. I've missed many a duck because of these fancy, expensive metals and alloys.

"Bismuth is thirty percent lighter than lead, so you use a bigger pellet which means fewer pellets per shell. Got it? Some swear it's only ten percent lighter than lead. Not.

"Guys have gone to steel #1s and #2s, but I reckon that's too few pellets. With Hevi-shot, you go from #6s to #4s, from three-hundred pellets per shell to less than a hundred and fifty. And those

---

[4] "My autoloader let the third shell slip past the carrier and jam the gun. I had to use a pocket knife to extract the jammed shell. My expensive shotgun was single-shot. I don't ever remember cursing the immortal soul of an unknown shotgun designer in quite the same way. I sold the gun when I got back." Smith, p. 82.

[5] "Tule Lake biologists, comparing shooting steel to an electronic shooting gallery where the birds drop as soon as you pull the trigger, convinced me that shooting directly at the birds is the best approach with steel shot. During the next hour, my opinion of steel shot was dramatically changed. Once a feel for the speed of the shot was developed, I found that the birds were easy to hit. I have been a firm believer in the effectiveness of steel shot ever since." Fletcher, p. 60.

"Don't worry, they're shooting
copper coated."

shells are two bucks a piece.

"That tungsten-iron stuff is heavier—closer to lead—but even *more* expensive than bismuth . . . and two or three times the cost of steel. I've considered shooting 18K gold, but the feds haven't approved it.

"Remington, Winchester, Federal or what, I don't give a damn. I just know that special shot ruined many a good duck hunt. It's ultimately good for the waterfowl, of course, but you can't expect any success with this non-lead alloy stuff."[6]

Version #4: Donnie Brought Wrong Loads

"Donnie took the shells with him last week and was supposed to bring 'em back this morning. We get out to the blind and he's brought the wrong shell box . . . #8s light load. You can't shoot a light load #8 at a duck! We'd have done great if any bobwhite or ruby throated hummingbirds had jumped up from the middle of the decoys. As it was, we didn't get a thing."

Version #5 Couldn't Hit a Thing[7,8,9,10,11]

"We just shot bad, that's all. Couldn't hit a thing. We got a look at some birds, but we got nada, zilch."

---

[6] Memphian and avid waterfowler B. Lee Mallory reports that the Illinois Department of Natural Resources, working with the Mississippi Flyway Council, indicated that during the 1996 / 1997 season nearly 1.4 million ducks were saved from toxic lead poisoning by the change to non-lead types of shot.

[7] "I did just about everything right, except shoot straight. After learning more about steel shot, I would have gone home early on a day like this. The ingredients of success here were foggy weather, an isolated spot, and locating the exact stop where ducks wanted to land. After a few minutes, two gadwall worked in over the tules. At twenty yards, I pulled up: boom . . . miss, boom . . . miss, boom. This was a record day . . . four missed shots. I had recorded eleven straight misses. Two more gadwall appeared. Boom . . . miss, boom . . . miss. However, it had been a good day. I'd seen plenty of wild life, and had more than enough chances." Fletcher, p. 55.

"But I'm shooting steel shot."

---

[8] "Leaping up, my parka hood covered my eyes. Suddenly, hay went everywhere. In my panic to get the geese that were so close, I should have held my fire. I missed two shots and the second shell failed to eject cleanly. By the time I cleared the gun and the third shot was chambered, the geese were out of range." Fletcher, p. 63.

[9] "Once the hunter establishes a pattern of missing ducks, it is very difficult to get back on the right track. That's one of the reasons it pays to be selective." Fletcher. P. 72.

[10] "It is astonishing how much room there is in the air around a duck. I have seen times when the birds were so thick that it seemed impossible to shoot a charge of shot through them without killing one or more, but how very easy it is to spare their lives." Grinnell, p. 389

[11] "I have never yet shot in a blind with a remarkably good shot. I know that there are such men, but it has never been my fortune to see one of them shooting wildfowl." Grinnell, p. 398.

"Forget the geese. Here comes the bull!"

Clothing and Camouflage[1]

Deception and disguise are critical elements of a successful hunt. When proper care is not taken to conceal the hunter, he is going to end up unsuccessful. Thus, the entire area of concealment provides great excuses for failure.

Version #1: Bad Costume Selection

"Sammy sees this flooded pasture *absolutely* covered up with ducks. And there, moving in, around and through the middle of these ducks is a bunch of cows. . . . I mean, right among 'em.

"These ducks are totally ignoring the cows, and the cows are totally ignoring the ducks. They're all happy out there feeding together.

"So Sammy, in his typically brilliant fashion, calls me at three-thirty in the morning and says, "Hey, I got it!" What he got was the idea that we dress up as a cow and sneak up on those ducks. By sneakin' right up on top of them disguised as a cow, Sammy figures we'll get a couple of dozen before they clear out.

"So he makes this cow suit. I can't image where he got that

---

[1] "The clothes a hunter wears and the personal equipment he carries have a considerable effect upon his pleasure and even his success afield; in no other hunting do they play so vital a role as in wildfowl gunning. In extreme cases, they can mean the difference between life and death." Janes, page 129.

cow skin.[2] "Well, this skin is complete with the hair, the head and horns . . . everything.

"Well, we park the truck way up the road, crawl down near the pasture and Sammy gets in the front of this cow costume and, needless to say, since it's his danged cow skin, I get the back end.

"Anyway, we're creeping up, step by step, ever so slowly on what must be a thousand ducks. We know it might take us an hour or more to get on 'em, if we do right, slow and cautious like. We've been easing along about twenty minutes and my knees and back are killing me from being all hunched over, all I'm seeing is Sammy's butt.

"Well then, I start pounding Sammy on the back saying 'let's get outta here'. Sammy says, 'quit it, we're almost there', and I say, 'Never mind, *I'm* the one who's in the back and here's comes the bull! And he's in an *amorous* state of mind!"[3]

Version #2 Clothes[4,5]

"Nope, we didn't even get a shot. Jimmy brought his boss and he'd never hunted before. How many times did I say, "Jimmy, make sure this guy is totally covered up in Mossy Oak. So, he shows up with that bright orange deer hunter stuff. I was really pissed and told him so. Anyway, we threw on top of him a bunch of cedar

---

[2] Sammy's the one who came up with two gallons of John-Deere-green paint at two a.m. when we were at State, so we could paint the dean's black BMW for our senior prank. It seemed like it was going to be funny at the time, but neither the college, the district attorney, or the judge seemed agree. But that's another story about jail time and fines and stuff. Anyway, we've always been impressed Sammy's creativity and improvisation.

[3] "Sometimes geese and brant are hunted with horses; a horse is trained to feed gradually up near to the flocks, and the gunner walks behind him until within range." Grinnell, p. 376

[4] "Since ducks are not color-blind, avoid wearing any loud shades." Smith, p. 102

[5] "If we could remain perfectly motionless, perhaps a splotch of color in our costumes wouldn't bother the ducks, but it seems humanly impossible to do so when birds are overhead." Janes, p. 31.

branches, found a moldy old tarp which we tossed over him, and told him to stay hunkered down in the corner of the blind. But old boss man just kept flaring the ducks, anyway. By the way, I meant to call Jimmy today and ask him what it's like to be out of work."

Version #3: The Blind[6,7]

"We're hunting a cornfield, and Prescott brings cedars and evergreens for our camouflage. Ridiculous. Aren't the ducks gonna wonder why there's a Christmas tree growing in the middle of a cornfield?"

Version #4: Wrong Camo[8]

"I told Pete to get Mossy Oak. He needed *Shadow Grass*™, but does he listen? Nooooo, he says we need some crap called advantage 4hd or seclusion or something. Last time they saw us every time. This morning, we stuck out like we were wearing bright orange and waving Old Glory.

"We used *Shadow Grass*™ last week and did great . . . perfect match with the dried rushes/cornstalks. Couple of weeks ago, we were huntin' some different stuff and we all agreed to wear our *Mossy Oak Brush*™, and we limited out in no time flat. Mike even got his wife to make a dog coat for the lab out of *Brush*™.

"I'll tell you what . . . these guys like to assume they're invisible,

---

[6] "Earlier, the ducks had seen me in the tules just as they came into range, and continually flared just before the shot. This led to much frustration and many missed shots. This time I selected a different patch of tules for my blind." Fletcher. p. 70.

[7] "First, concealment is critical. The vegetation used to disguise the blind should be of materials native to that area, and of the same age as surrounding vegetation. Using dead brown cattails while gunning early fall teal is a dead giveaway. Likewise, cornstalks among the reeds labels you a beginner." Smith, p. 29

[8] "The color of the vegetation can be significant, if it doesn't blend with the color of the hunters' camouflage." Fletcher, p. 75.

"Man, you can't wear 'Winter Marsh Grass' camo in a flooded rice field."

but it don't work that way. You have got to do your camo homework
. . . you have to wear the right stuff.

"We'd have taken a lot of ducks, if we'd picked the right camo
for this morning, but man, the ducks just kept flaring at our stuff.
If those guys don't start wearing *Mossy Oak*™, well I might start
wearing QuackMyAssGrass."

"John, don't you think little Johnny
might rather be home watching some
animal channel on TV?."

Guests and Companions[1]

*S*ome hunters consider it a good day if their companion doesn't shoot a hole in the boat, the dog, or the guide. Others set pretty high standards, demanding their cohorts be, well, almost as good as themselves. Duck hunting associates always cause problems . . . relentless in their pursuit of you having a terrible day.

Version # 1: Billy Brought His Son—Basic[2]

"I told him the boy would have to behave, right? But no. He jumped around every time we got some birds. Spooked 'em good, that boy did."

Version #2: Billy Brought His Son—Advanced (Billy's Son Dropped His Mug of Hot Chocolate)

"The only birds we seen all day—working good—and Billy's boy stood up—I told him to sit down—and he drops a whole cup of hot chocolate on himself and me. It was a mess. And the chocolate lab was really *chocolate*. But ducks don't like spilled hot chocolate."

---

[1] "A lack of basic duck hunting knowledge and skills results in higher wounding losses, conflicts between hunters in the field, and a value system that places greater emphasis on the kill than on the experience." Concerned Duck Hunters Panel.

[2] "Your bright shining face may have won you your life's mate, but it scares the hell out of ducks. Use a face mask. Movement is a factor as well. When people move, it shows." Hinman p. 171.

Version #3: Kept Looking Up[3,4]

"Ducks can see a man's face from eight or twelve miles away. You have to keep your head down and your bright white face covered up. Larry doesn't have much hunting experience . . . kept looking straight up, flaring every every duck. We didn't shoot a thing."[5,6]

Version #4: Shot at Wrong Duck[7,8]

"Chester doesn't have much experience at this sort of thing. We're sitting in the blind like we always sit and a brace of ducks comes from our right. Well, when birds cross the decoys right to left, the left gunner takes the lead bird, so you're not shooting across yourselves. Well, these woodies[9] cross our decoys and bang, bang . . . nothing falls. Chester then tells me he shot at the drake on the left. I say 'you dummy, we were shooting at the same bird.' He says

---

[3] "The shores of Long Island Sound looked like a daisy field with all the white faces of the gunners peering up at him as he flew by . . . at over a thousand feet—not at two hundred." *Duck Hunting* by Frank MacKenty, A.S. Barnes & Co., 1953. p. 142.

[4] "Some duck hunters have a pernicious habit, becoming imbued with the idea that the seventh inning occurs about six times every hour and they get itchy-tail and have to stand up. Thereupon—in about one out of three stand-ups—a small snarl of ducks tries to visit your stool and, of course, flares away." MacKenty, p. 148.

[5] "Ducks possess excellent vision, and the higher the degree of edibility of a species of duck, the better its vision and the greater its capacity for alarm and apprehension." MacKenty, p. 8.

[6] "So many times I have seen ducks headed straight for the stool until someone in the blind lifted his head and the flash of white of his face showed through or over the blind dressing." MacKenty, p. 141.

[7] "Hunters must understand the nuances of shooting at a flock of divers. The man closer to the front of the flock—the person on the right, if the birds approach from the right—should work on the birds at the end of the flock; his partner should take the leaders. This is a good technique because it ensures that both men will have shooting." Smith, p. 86.

[8] "(The hunters) didn't handle the choosing of targets correctly. They took the front-end ducks first. They should have waited until all the birds were in range, taken their first shots at the tailenders, and then mopped up the closer birds last." Smith, p. 128.

[9] Nickname for the Wood duck. The Linnean name is *Aix sponsa*.

"I <u>told</u> you to leave that phone
in the truck!."

'Whatever, I didn't see you drop any.' Chester will confuse you like that. Anyway, birds cross like that and the right man just has to take the trailing bird, that's all. How could that have been my fault?"

"If you're going to accept an invitation to go hunting, the least you could do is learn a little about how it's done, so you don't make your host go duckless."

Version #5: Bobby Ray Overslept

"Dang that boy, anyway! Bobby Ray overslept again. He was supposed to pick us up at 4:15. By the time we got loaded up and got to the boat, it was already sunrise. You can forget it by then . . . it takes too long to get to the blind, and set up. We might as well stayed in altogether. Un-danged-reliable, that's what Bobby Ray is. I tell you what, if he didn't own the boat, the decoys, and the blind, we wouldn't hunt with him anyway."

Version #6: Shells Flared the Birds[10]

"We get three early passes, each time it looks like the birds are going to come in and then they flare. By the time it calms down, we haven't fired a shot and I look over by Eph, and he's got his bright shiny shells all red and brass lined up on the top of the blind. No wonder the birds flared. You just can't do that . . . the birds see that and hightail it out of there."

Version #7: Got Lost

"Lonnie says, 'Hey, I found this great new place only a half mile from 20,000 acres of bean and rice fields . . . ducks and geese everywhere.'

"Knowing Lonnie's 'eccentricities', I suggest getting there two hours before dawn. "Two hours!" Lonnie howls, but finally relents.

---

[10] "If you think that the ducks may have seen you, they probably did," Fletcher, p.11

"I thought <u>you</u> brought the shells."

Unfortunately, he forgot a couple of things: his boots, headlamp, flashlight, compass, map . . . little stuff, you know. We spend forty five minutes driving down gravel roads, him saying every minute, 'Yeah, here it is . . . I remember this levee.' Mind you, every levee we passed for the past eighteen miles looked the same. Finally Lonnie shouts, 'This is it! I remember that old tractor tire over there.' You guessed it, we'd passed about ten dozen old tractor tires in the past hour.

"Convinced he's finally got the right place, we load up our gear, equipment, dogs, a couple of dozen decoys and begin our trek through the Delta gumbo, mud sticking in ten pound globs to our waders. Wet from sweat after about a mile painful slog, Lonnie starts muttering under his breath, 'Uh, uh, uh, ummm, uh, ummm', at which point I know we're closer to a Wendy's, than any ducks.

"Damn, Lonnie, are you sure you got the right *state?*" By the time the sun is full in the sky, he admits he's got no idea where we are and suggests maybe he should have taken some notes, made a map, or come back to the place at night to make sure he could find it.

"We did meet a couple of nice farmers, though all things considered, we'd have preferred that they didn't call the wardens, police, *and* county sheriff. Anyway, I did find out that trespassing brings a pretty reasonable fine, especially when Lonnie pays for both of us."

Version #8: Left Too Soon[11,12]

"Sonny had to get home early for his daughter's soccer game . . . like she's Mia Hamm or something, I guess. Sonny knows that birds

---

[11] "Another common mistake is the reluctance to stay out long enough to give your rig a chance. Some of my very best shooting always comes within a few minutes of the end of legal shooting time. The lesson is to wait it out." Smith, p. 130.
[12] "It was still early in the day—only 2 o'clock—time yet to kill a lot of birds." Grinnell, p. 390.

around here don't start working until late, but he makes other arrangements anyway. We left too soon. As we're coming in, tons of birds over the tree line are starting to work. Just like I said. We hadn't left so soon, we'd had a limit.

"Everybody likes to be out there at first light for that early-morning flurry of birds. Then things slow to a trickle or stop. Lots of hunters head home . . . leave too soon. You wait, you get the next wave of action. Lots of activity between ten in the morning and two in the afternoon sometimes. That's only four more hours of sitting. Then comes the second major flight, from three until sunset.

"Most places are hunted lightly in the afternoon, ours included. Prime time to hit those December birds that've been feeding inland, heading to open water late in the day for drink and sleep.

"Sonny says he's going to get to have the head of his daughter's soccer league get the rest of her games scheduled for weeknights. That'll work."

Version #9: Ezra Misunderstood the Term "Stool"

"Ezra was new to duck hunting when we asked him to jump out of the blind and 'take care of the stool'. That was the last we saw of him. It occurred to us after a few hours that we might should oughta have used the term 'decoys' or 'set', but by then Ezra was long gone. Jimmy later got a message from Ezra saying he wasn't participating in any sport where he had to mess around with someone else's stools."

There is much myth and misunderstanding regarding the duck hunting term "stool". The dictionary says: 1. a simple seat without a back or arms; 2. solid excretory product evacuated from the bowels 3. to lure with a stool, as of wild fowl; 4. react to a decoy of wildfowl. Many years ago, hunters used a pigeon—or sometimes

"Got any more secret spots?"

a "dummy" of a pigeon to decoy birds.[13] Encarta reports that "hunters' decoys were originally tied to a wooden platform." The American English Dictionary cites a 1830 source explaining that the term 'stool', meaning a set of duck decoys, "is said to be from the notion of decoys fastened to stools to lure other pigeons. From the Online Dictionary: "But perhaps related to stall 'decoy bird' (1500), especially a pigeon used to entice a hawk into the net."

It seems sure that "stool" is derived from pigeon decoys, thus linking the duck hunting "stool" to the term "stool pigeon", used to describe an informer spying for the police.

As an example, Jim Low writes in *The Missouri Conservationist*, 'To a novice, one decoy spread looks pretty much like another. But designing a stool that pulls ducks in is an art.'

The ducking-stool was a contrivance whereby scolding or drunken women were ducked in a pond. However, the use of the words "duck" and "stool" in this sense is coincidental, since this use refers to the tying of an alleged miscreant to a wooden stool and dunking them into water.

Version #10: Jimmie Had a Bad Sign for Today

"I don't know why Jimmie has to read his horrorscope. Makes no sense to me, because every time he does, our shooting is downright

---

[13] "The finishing touch was to set out the live decoys—three in number, two ducks and a drake. For each live decoy there is a "stool", which consists of a sharpened stick 2 feet long, surmounted by a circular or oval piece of board 6 inches across. Fastened to the stick which supports this board is a leather line 3 feet long and terminating in two loops, which are slipped over the duck's two feet and drawn tight so that the bird cannot get away, yet not so tight as to press unduly on the flesh. John pushed the point of one of the duck stools into the mud until the little table on which the bird was to stand was 2 inches below the water's surface. I studied the live decoys which were having a very good time, washing themselves and preening, occasionally tipping up to feed on the bottom. After a while each swam to its stool and clambered on it, standing there and arranging its feathers." Grinnell, p. 548.

lousy. He shouldn't buy newspapers in the TigerMart . . . just messes up our hunts. This morning his horroscope says, 'Beware of flying objects. Outdoor activities will present challenges.' If Jimmie would stop buying that ass-trology stuff, we'd finally get a good hunt."

Version #11: Ronnie's Stove[14]

"Nothing like a stove to keep you warm during bitter cold days . . . and to dry socks or gloves or anything uncomfortably wet, i.e. everything. Yup, nothing like a stove, unless it's Ronnie's. He's got propane, kerosene, butane, charcoal briquettes, fire-starter logs, designer matches . . . everything . . . other than the New York City Fire Department! First, he's fussing with fire before we get settled, and flares three braces. After a few hot coals fall out and burn through the floor of the blind, we catch that distinctive smell of burning rubber, in this case our hunting boots, melting off our feet. Finally, Ronnie sets fire to the entire side of the blind. Ever seen dry cedar branches and corn stalks go up in flame? We barely got out alive, jumping into the water, scrambling to the boat and watching, shivering cold, as our blind burned flat with flames twenty feet high. Before the fire, Crenshaw said he'd rather freeze than put up with Ronnie's stove. He got his wish."

---

[14] "They wear thick warm clothing. They take lunches and sometimes carry small stoves in boat or blind to warm their food or themselves if the weather becomes too bad. But with all these added comforts has come one great drawback which outweighs them all, the scarcity of waterfowl." Grinnell, p. 242.

"The next one to cook beans in camp
gets shot on sight. . .
<u>and</u> banished from the club."

"Sure there's enough water.
Now, get ready! I think Bo has spotted
some birds!"

Water[1]

Water *is pretty darned important to a duck. After all, they are* water*fowl, and the places they hang out are* wet*lands.*

Version #1: Too Little Water

"There's not enough water. There's no places to rest, nowhere to feed. Our blind is sitting high and dry. Ducks aren't going to come until we get some real water. I'll tell you what happened today . . . we got skunked."

Version #2: Too much Water[2]

"Too much water right now . . . ducks can go anywhere and just sit. With water everywhere, no way to get 'em up."

Version #3: Need Rain[3]

"Hunting's been terrible all around. Some people had a great

---

[1] It is difficult to do justice to all of the water excuses available. We just skim the surface, so to speak, of the great mass of lame excuses one might derive from this category.

[2] "In this northern habitat, water is no problem—except there is sometimes too much!" Wesley, ed. p. 26.

[3] "Within this area are the deltas of the great northern rivers, whose shallow lakes support waterfowl populations. Here, the major limiting factor to production is widely fluctuating water levels." Wesley, ed. p. 29.

early season, but it's tapered off and a limit of anything is hard to come by. Heck, yesterday I couldn't get a limit of blackbirds. Up north, I think they got some rain. We need rain, bad. We've got plenty of weather, we need rain."

Version #4: Dry Up North

"Rainfall was way down in Saskatchewan, the Dakotas, and every place else. Early-nesting birds like mallards just overflew the breeding grounds and headed into Canada's bush country. When ducks over-fly the prairies before nesting season, we end up with zero ducks."

"If we want to get ducks, we're gonna
need more water."

Calling

*C*alling offers great reasons to blame others. No two hunters ever agree on the quality of another's calling. Just remember, everyone but you is terrible at calling.

Version #1: Not Enough Calling

"They wouldn't call. Me, I'm blowing away, but you have to have more sound . . . a lot of voices . . . like a lot of ducks, particularly for high ones. With the wind and all, you just got to keep working at it. It tires you out, blowing like that, but you have to do it that way. You can't go light on calling under those conditions and expect to get ducks."

Version #2: Too Much Calling[1]

"How are we going to get ducks with Bobby blowing his damned call all the time? These birds are smart. They been called at by experts and amateurs down the flyway. Too much calling just puts them off."

---

[1] "Calling dabbling ducks is usually a matter of too much at the wrong time. Calling is an inexact science. For it to work, you've got to understand waterfowl mentality. Specifically, to understand when calling will and will not work. The insistence that some hunters have for calling right until the birds hit the water frequently flares birds that otherwise would have set down." Smith p. 27

Version #3: Bad Calling[2,3]

"Reggie bought a friend who sounded like a gay brant with Montezuma's revenge! How can you get ducks when you sound like a drunk Scotchman playing 'Stand By Your Man' on the bagpipes with a zucchini up his kiester."

Version #4: Bad Calls[4,5]

"I told Bobby, bring your Rich n' 'Tone, your Carlson, your Olt . . . hell, bring that Cocobola tree thing, but for God's sake don't bring that thing you whittled in your basement. *Herter's, Bryant, Faulk, Beauchamp* are fine, but don't bring anything homemade.

"Last time, Bobby brought that thing, we got two coots and a spoonie. Might as well whistle Brooks and Dunn outta your butt in E Minor as have Bobby screeching like a maniac with that call."

---

[2] "You cannot blow a call like a New Year's Eve horn after the eighth drink." MacKenty, p. 58.

[3] "To the novice, most mystifying is that successful calling seldom sounds like a duck. This is not to say it can't, just that many styles of calling do not, even though they produce deadly results." Hinman, p.174.

[4] Just the creativity in names proves the importance of calling: *Nasty II, Fusion Wench, Jezebel, Tall Timber, Migrators Legend, Double Reed Squealer, Duck Commander, Brown Sugar, Camo Big Talker, Mallard Magic, Timber Rattler, Daisy Cutter, Quack Stacker, Nasty Boy* and *P.H.A.T Lady Call.* Two favorites are *The Poison,* and *Yo' Sister Call.*

[5] "Most calls put me in mind of an infamous Whoopee Pillow of the Gay Twenties, operated by a two-hundred-pound victim." MacKenty, p. 51.

Version #5: Using Wrong Call[6]

"You have to use the right call at the right time. It's not a matter of life and death, it's more important than that. If you use the right call at the wrong time, or the wrong call at the right time, you're not going to get ducks, see? And you can't use the wrong call at the wrong time, either.

The chart below will help the duck hunter understand the consequences of improper choice of kind of call and the right time to use it.

Time To Use Call

Wrong Call at the Wrong Time = Certain Failure
Wrong Call at the Right Time = Ducks Leave the Country
Right Call at the Wrong Time = Certain Failure
Right Call at the Right Time = Never Happens

"You got a highball call—folks mistakenly call it a 'hail', it's your loud attention getter.

"The 'comeback' call is like the highball, except it's softer, shorter, and more pleading. Then you got the 'greeting' call, which is kind of like a cheerful hello.

"Then there's a couple of hen calls. Drakes and hens sound

---

[6] Consider that there are four hundred and fifty eight different duck species in North America and different calls for drake and hen. This totals 916 different calls. Then, each duck has 6.74 calls each, e.g. feeding, dating, mating, just-plain-happy, stress, etc. Thus, all told, there are over 6,176 separate and discrete calls to master, excluding important differences in tone and sound between young and old ducks. Fortunately, manufacturers have developed a separate call for each.

different, because of the differences in their trachea and syrinx.[7] The mallard hen's got a short two-syllable qu-ACK, that sounds happy . . . your 'I'm happy' hen call . . . which, of course, is why they call it the 'happy call'.

"Then you got the 'lonesome hen'. The Lonesome Hen comes from your basic quack, but it's spaced wide, real nasal and drawn out. If your quacks are too close together, it'll scare the ducks . . . got to be low and throaty, see?

"Then there's the 'pleading' call . . . folks call the 'begging hail'. It's kind of a Kaanc, Kaanc, Kanc, Kanc type sound . . . for real long calls on difficult ducks. (Like they all aren't difficult!)

"Well, you guessed it. All morning long, these guys are hailing when they should be highballing; chattering instead of chuckling; and pleading when they should be greeting. It was a real mess. Only a deaf duck would dared come close, and there weren't any hearing-impaired ducks out there all morning.

"Just have to vocalize proper, that's all."

Version #6: Calling Over Ice

"There's a particular way to call over ice. Mostly, you control your volume and get softer. That means wearing a heavy glove on your holding hand, using a timber call. And when you're hunting geese, you have to switch from a short reed call to a flute call. You have to sound mellow. The ice ricochets your sound. Not good. Plus, you got to switch to less aggressive cadences, more relaxed. Short and simple . . . contented quacks, chuckles and greetings.

---

[7] The syrinx is the duck's vocal organ, consisting of thin vibrating muscles close to the division of the trachea in the bronchi. There are documented cases of hunters being thrown from a blind for actually using the word 'syrinx' in a sentence. Unless you have a Cornell doctoral degree in ornithological bioacoustics, the author recommends eschewing use of the term 'syrinx'.

"These boys don't hunt over ice much here. Having ice is a whole new ball game. No, we didn't get anything with them boys not knowing how to call when there's ice."

Version #7: The Starks Boys Didn't Show Up and Neither Did Calef[8,9]

"Everybody knew we'd need expert calling, so we were expecting a couple of Starks boys. They never showed and the rest of us just scared off the ducks."

Version #8: Competitors' Calling[10]

"The guys in the next blind screwed things up.[11] Cowboys, that's what they were. I haven't ever heard a chuckle, highball, chatter, comeback and greeting—*all at the same time.* They sounded like Palestinian funeral wailers on meth. Those guys chased away everything from Suisun City to Cibola."

---

[8] "Down South, duck calling has attained to the dignity of a fine art and the professional caller to the stature of a concert violinist. At Stuttgart, the country's top callers compete for the world championship. Contestants display incredible ability in giving out with duck talk and these same men in the bayous and river bottoms of their native Southland perform prodigies with the reed each autumn." Janes, p. 55.

[9] Of the 70 or so National Duck Calling Championships, all held in Stuttgart, 18 winners have been from Stuttgart, and a total of 23 from the state. There have been 9 winners from Iowa, the next best showing. Mike McLemore, Ed Holt and Jake Gartner have each won three times. John Liston, Herb Parsons, Pat Peacock, W.C. Cross, Harry Wieman, and Ken McCullum have each won twice. The Starks have three victories, split between Mike (1) and David (2).

[10] "If the guy next to you is continuously blaring away, then you want to consider finding another location." Fletcher, p. 10.

[11] "There is a maxim that 'the guy in the other blind is a son-of-a-bitch.' If the hunters in the adjacent blind are obnoxious, change your decoy set-up to the far side of the blind. However, obnoxiousness is frequently due more to ignorance than malice." Hinman, p. 193.

Dog[1]

C anis lupis familiaris *has been bred to perform specific tasks, among them jumping on people and getting into the trash. But the most important task, after guns have been fired and ducks downed, is for the dog to hurl himself into freezing water, swim around aimlessly for an eternity, and return to the blind, shake bitterly cold water on you, and look up adoringly.*

Version #1: No Dog

"Johnny's lab, 'Tuffguy', got sick last night. Not so "tuff", it seems to me. Johnny thinks he gave him too many Cheetoes, either that or Ding Dongs, he's not exactly sure. I think it was the Slim Jims. I know a dog can eat a three or four dozen, but more than that, and you're *asking* for trouble.

"Tuffguy is chubby, but he's a very fine retriever. Where we hunt, we can't do anything without him. Can't take long shots, or we'll lose all the cripples.

"I admit, I don't miss one bit that dog's fartin' in the blind— got to be the *Slim Jims*—but we can't really a bird without him."

---

[1] "If you have a poorly trained or untrained dog and insufficient gunning time to train him, you had better leave him at home, for he can be more trouble than he is worth, and your gunning expedition will degenerate into either a nursery school for the dog or a remedial course in dog gunning manners." MacKenty, p. 150

"That dog never comes back
empty-handed."

Version #2: Bad Dog[2,3,4]

"Mike says he's a labrador, and I know for a fact that Mike paid good money for him. But if he's a lab, he sure was designed by a committee. Dog isn't worth a pint of panther piss, jumping all around, knocking over shell boxes, crapping in the blind . . . the dog from hell, I tell you . . . Cujo of the Marsh, that's what.

"For some damn reason, Walter brings a trap grade, thirty-inch Beretta . . . showing off a $20,000 gun, I guess. Well, we're sitting around, talking, drinking coffee and such, and low and behold, the whole time that lab is chewing the forearm of Walter's Beretta. This is an 'all original parts' gun and the dog is eating it for breakfast. That'll cost Walter a few grand.

"The cursed dog wouldn't go get a duck. Probably full from eating Walter's gun. It's hard to swim on a full stomach, especially if it's full with fine grained wood, so I didn't blame the dog. Of course, we struck out this morning."

Version #3: Dog Too Young

"I'm sorry, but you can't bring a young dog like Tommy did. There's no damned sense bringing a pup without a clue about what he's doing. Tommy claims it's a dog. Billy thought it was a cat that somehow Tommy taught to bark and jump around like a dog. That alleged dog retrieved like a cat, anyway. You can't bring a young dog out hunting. You got to get him *right* first. And that dog—or

---

[2] "A dog creates a multitude of problems when hunting on a refuge. The problems include: fighting with other dogs, not staying in the blind, retrieving other hunters' ducks, disappearing into the dark when going or coming from the field." Fletcher, p. 18

[3] "When a dog moves, it shows. It is imperative to stay still." Smith. p. 129.

[4] The dog climbs into the boat, and with muddy feet and dripping hide, carefully squats upon the middle seat every time, provided they were wet and muddy. We argued with him to no purpose." Grinnell, p. 348

whatever it was—was not *right*. We would have had ducks, weren't for that young dog."

"He might be a little young, but he's got to learn sometime."

Version #4: Dog Too Old

There comes a time when you gotta leave old' Jake, Buck, or whatever the hell his name is, at home. Jerry Rae even thinks he can bring his incontinent dog. At least Jerry Rae doesn't pee on the shell bag *and* the lunch at the *same time*. Both Jerry Rae and Spad should've stayed home.[5] Spad's just too old. He can't see the birds, can't smell, can't hear 'em. One time, to make fun of old Spad, Jimmie brought a pair of dark glasses, a cane and a diaper to the hunt . . . and Jerry Rae thought that they were for *him*. An old dog can ruin a hunt just by everyone feeling sorry for him. We sure didn't feel sorry for Jerry Rae, when he threw out his back lifting Spad in and out of the boat."

---

[5] Every guy with a chocolate lab names him Mocha, Hershey, Cappuchio, Starbuck, Chestnut, Cinnamon, UPS, Nestle, Ginger, Brownie, Coffee, or Cocoa. Jerry Rae called his dog 'spadiceous', some rare word meaning chestnut-brown. We honored the brown color-naming legacy by referring to Jerry Rae's dog as 'crap brain', 'dump head', 'warm pile', 'feces', and 'you dumb shit, go get the goddam bird'.

Version #5: Not Throwing the Dog High Enough

"After striking out last week, the guy at the feed store said we had to have a dog. So we got one. But we still didn't get any ducks. I told Tommy I thought that he just wasn't throwin' the dog high enough."

Version #6: Brought Back Wrong Ducks

"Kenny's retriever got out there all right. He jumped right into the water and grabbed a decoy, struggled to get a hold on it, swam back and dropped it at our feet, line, weight and all. We didn't get any ducks, but by the end of the morning, we did have nine decoys in our blind."

"I told you he was good with ducks."

Version #7: Dog Wouldn't Go Out on the Ice[6]

"Why would a dog would even consider going into cold water? Humans aren't worth the trouble, but I guess no one ever explained that to them. Anyway, Wilson calls his dog 'stupid' because the dog refuses to retrieve around ice. I call him smart. Anyway, we couldn't hardly shoot; no way to get the downed ducks."

"So, he doesn't like to get wet... but he's still a great retriever."

---

[5] "I have seen a dog lie down on his belly with widely spread forelegs and drag himself along inch by inch, this spreading his weight over as great a surface as possible so as to avoid breaking through thin ice. Once, a bird fell heavily on thin ice, breaking through and not reappearing. The dog found the hole in the ice, but not the duck. Then, he stopped 3 or 4 feet from the hole, began to scratch, making a small hole and, quickly enlarging it, put his mouth down into the water, pulled out the duck and brought it to shore." Grinnell, p. 409.

The precise time that ducks come in.

Freddie Eliminating

very hunter knows ducks possess some eerie extrasensory perception enabling them to discern when a hunter abandons his guard to perform one of nature's most basic tasks. After sitting for hour after hour, a hunter has only to drop his boots and pull down three layers of pants and the sky comes alive with ducks.

Version #1: Freddie Taking a Pee

"So, the only ducks we see come while Freddie's out of the blind taking a pee. It always happens with him.

"You shouldn't drink beer at five o'clock in the morning anyway. It's a *safety* issue. *Drinking and guns never mix.*

"Freddie, he takes a sip of coffee, then sips beer. Before you know it, he's out of the blind taking a leak. His pee breaks are perfectly timed to coincide with the arrival of ducks. It happened four or five times. That man needs a bladder twice the size of a normal man, or some sort of catheter thing."

Version #2: Freddie Taking a Dump

"So, the only ducks we see all morning come around while Freddie's out of the blind taking a dump. It always happens with him. Damn, he's either gotta change his diet or find someone new to hunt with.

"I mean, what can you say about a guy whose two favorite cuisines are Mexican and Indian, and his absolute favorite is mixing up the two. You haven't lived until you've shared a duck blind with a guy who ate a curry biryani taco the previous night.

"Twenty greenheads made a single pass and headed straight in all cupped up, but just out of range. And Freddie's out there wiping his behind with a corn stalk, yelling and cursing. Jimmy still swears he could hear those ducks laughing. Those were the only ducks we saw all day."

Hunting Pressure

So many duck hunters whine about not killing ducks, it's amazing that legions still, week after week, continue their masochistic quest. Nevertheless, the faithful keep banging away, thereby creating their own failure—too many hunters chasing too few ducks . . . and it's always the other guy's fault.,

Version #1: Too Many Hunters[1,2,3]

"Today, we're hunting fewer and fewer birds, with less and less wetlands, spread over many more hunters, in every flyway. The secret to more ducks is simple: fewer hunters ."

---

[1] Sales of Federal Migratory Bird Hunting and Conservation Stamps ('Duck Stamps') provide a proxy for hunter numbers. (Some who buy stamps don't hunt; some who hunt ducks don't buy the stamp, an illegal practice, by the way. Numbers of stamp-buying non-hunters and non-stamp-buying hunters are statistically insignificant.) Duck Stamp sales indicate that hunters who complain about 'too many hunters' are off base. From around a half million in its early years in the 1930s, Duck Stamp sales grew to 1.4 million a year in the mid- to late-1940s. By 1964, annual sales had fallen to 1.1 million, only to rise to a record 2.4 million in 1973. Recent years have been around 1.5 million.

[2] "Next to clear weather, the biggest duck hunting curse is overcrowding. On these days, the best option is to just stay home." Fletcher. p. 68.

[3] "The major thing to avoid is another hunter set up directly down wind of you. A pleasant conversation with your neighbors prior to shooting time is well worth the effort in that it creates a work together atmosphere rather than a competition." Fletcher, p.90.

Version #2: Public Hunting Area[4]

"Ducks in public marshes are worked hard. The birds adjust to the early morning routine, they clear out before sunrise . . . or just won't fly at all in the morning. The public launch was so crowded this morning, it looked like sale days at Wal-Mart."

Version #3: Over Hunted

"We put our time, money and effort into creating decent habitat that will draw and hold waterfowl, then we overhunt it. You put too much pressure on ducks, they leave. It doesn't take them long to figure that out. Think about this. If you got shot at in your driveway every day when you left for work and every day when you came home, wouldn't you move out of the neighborhood? I sure would."

Version #4: Shot Out

"Every area around here is covered up with hunters. By this time of year, I suppose you can't expect any ducks. This kind of hunting is taking your gun for a walk outdoors, that's all.

"The state guy said one of those aerial surveys showed that every blind along the floodplain was full up. Duck hunting's gotten too popular, he says. For some reason, it's become cool to duck hunt.

"In the 1960s, there weren't fifteen thousand duck hunters in this state . . . killing about fifty thousand ducks a year. Now we got twenty thousand hunters, and they kill *half a million* ducks a year.

"We didn't get ducks yesterday, not today and we're not going to get ducks tomorrow. How can we? Everything's just plain shot out."

---

[4] "Managed (public) areas are the hunting of the future. Supported with hunters' money, they are planned with waterfowl in mind. Hunting is controlled, and the sporting experience is what matters. Hunters are not jammed together, and limits on the number of shells discourages skybusting." Smith, p. 18.

Version #5: Birds Shot Over

"These birds have been shot over. I've never seen birds so skittish. Must've been those boys out here a couple of days ago. . . they did one heck of a lot of shootin' . . . spooked the birds, they did.

"They shot so much it sounded like a West Bank wedding reception. Somebody said that Winchester and Federal stock was up ten-percent the next day. No birds when they been shot over like this."

"Not bad, but I still prefer Parker Brothers and Purdeys."

Ivory Billed Woodpecker[1]

The discovery of the Ivory Billed Woodpecker
provides one of the most original excuses that has
come along in ages.

"For thirty years, we've hunted from Cotton Plant down to
Smale, from Hopper over to Pepper's Landing. Places that are
virtually impossible to get to, for human beings, that is. And
some of those places are absolutely *covered up* with ducks. We
had it all to ourselves.

"Then, the worst possible thing happens: they find the
Ivory Billed Woodpecker right smack dab in the middle of our
hunting grounds.

"Buddy Willis says he knows the difference between a Pileated
Woodpecker and an Ivory Billed. Says he's known for twenty years
that Ivory Billed thing was in there. He knows the difference in the
white wing pattern, the call, and the nesting and feeding habits of
each species.

"They found the woodpecker where Buddy usually sets up

---

[1] Long believed extinct—60 years since the last confirmed sighting—the Ivory-billed
Woodpecker was rediscovered in the Big Woods of eastern Arkansas—a vast area of bottomland swamp forest—in 2004 by Gene Sparling. The area consists of 550,000 acres of prime
duck hunting bayous, bottomland, forest and lakes.

during the season. Now, it's covered up with Ph.D.s from Cornell and every sort of ornitho-geek from around the country. Those woodpecker searchers rented every damned jon boat in Lee, St. Francis, Prairie, White, Woodruff and Phillips counties.

"He says he's going to take out the last of the Ivory Bills. My guess is that it's against the law. If it's not, seems like it should be. Local t-shirt and motel revenues are way up since they saw that bird.

"I understand how a bird like that can ruin a good hunt, and I can't deny that duck hunting is probably the most important thing in most people's lives, certainly in Buddy's. But with all that good tourism, I'd hate to see Buddy pop off that bird. He says no one would notice and, unfortunately, he's probably right.

"Buddy says he's even seen those big woodpeckers when he's been hunting the Atchafalaya basin in Louisiana. He called some bird people to report it and they asked him had he been drinking. He said, 'Sure, shots of Jagermeister and Red Bull . . . just like always . . . but that doesn't mean I didn't see that Ivory Billed.' They apparently told him to go make love to himself.

"Buddy's crazy, but he *lives* in those swamps. I don't have any idea what he's talking about most of the time, but one time, over a couple of Jager-bulls, as he calls his 'potion of preference', he leaned over the table, looked carefully over each shoulder, and whispered, 'Don't tell a soul, but they're back in the Singer Tract. If you say anything, that'll be ruined for duck hunting, too.'"

"Orange Mantle, Green Scapulars, Black Retrices, Red Coverts? They're either Fan-Tailed Widowbirds or Pied Barbets."

"Just shut up...it worked for the indians."

Decoys[1,2,3]

For all the fuss, there are plenty of folks who think decoys don't make a big difference. Don't make that mistake. If you get skunked, decoys provide rich opportunities for excuses. There are limitless adaptations of 'improperly setting the decoys'; this humble paper addresses only those which limited time and space allow. Decoy setting can provide an entire season of excuses for those willing to invest time in concocting excuses.

Version #1: Hens in Front of Drakes, Open Water:

"We just never did get the right set.[4] Johnny put the hens out in front of the drakes and didn't leave a pocket of open water. I tried to tell him, but would he listen? Noooooo . . . ."

---

[1] "Learn how to spread them properly, for a great deal depends upon the appearance of your spread. A poorly planned stool will fail to attract ducks on the best days, while a strategically arranged stool will usually pull in a stray duck or two on even the worst days." Janes, p. 77.

[2] Some variables of decoy setting: upwind v. downwind; number of decoys; species of decoy; gender of the duck; wide spacing versus tight spacing; placement of a pocket of open water for landing; the shape or arrangement of the decoys; magnum (oversized) decoys vs. regular; use of 'confidence' decoys; mix of goose and duck decoys, and placement thereof.

[3] The 2,000-year-old decoys discovered in Nevada's Lovelock Cave—the oldest existing examples-were fashioned by the Tule Indians in a manner typical of basket weaving of the period.

[4] "Set" is the arrangement of decoys which, we have learned, may also be referred to non-scatalogically, as the "stool".

Version #2: Too Few Decoys

"You need a big spread for these birds and we just didn't have enough decoys to attract 'em. You gotta have a lot to make a good impression (pick one): out here; down here; up here; over here. You really need (pick one): dozens; hundreds; thousand; millions of dekes to have any success. These birds have been shot over and they're not going to trust anything other than a huge spread."

Version #3: Confidence Decoy[5,6]

"I never believed in 'confidence' decoys. Stevie swears by them, but they're worth squat. Stevie has this Great Blue Heron decoy, and one day we're having no luck. So, Stevie puts out his heron decoy. That sealed it. Until then, at least we'd seen a lot of ducks. As soon as the heron goes out, we don't see another duck *all day*. I really hate it when he's got his seagull, coot, crows, snowy egret, and green-backed heron, all out at once with the great blue heron. Looks like a zoo out there . . . just scares the ducks off."

Version #4: Setup[7]

"Ducks over geese . . . never geese over ducks. That's the way it is . . . that's the way it's always been . . . that's the way it always will be.

"You learn when you're a little shaver that you got to keep your duck decoys and goose decoys separate, and arrange them so that

---

[5] "Placing a few seagull decoys at the head of our rig helps decoy wary ducks. They are highly visible, and seagulls frequently associate with waterfowl. However, don't place downwind of your set, because decoying ducks don't pass over other species." p. 27. *161 Waterfowling Secrets, Ducks Unlimited*, Editor, Globe Pequot Press, 1994.

[6] "To really fool that wary old suzy, try a great blue heron decoy as a sentinel." *161 Waterfowling Secrets* p. 32.

[7] Readers wishing to learn more about the subject should refer to the author's book, *Optimal Decoy Arrangements—Or How to Achieve Duck Hunting Success While Keeping Your Friends' Mouths Shut*, Pseudologos Publishing, copyright 2008.

"Maybe we should pick up and
move to the river..."

when they land, the geese don't have to come in over the ducks. Geese just won't land over top of ducks. But ducks will land over top of geese. The ducks just aren't picky like the geese are . . . and not as careful.

"Not only do you have to create the illusion you want, you've got to create a proper landing zone. The illusion's got to be properly thought out. Do you want the decoys to look like ducks that have just set down? Dabbling? Loafing? Feeding ducks? Do you want an 'X', a fishhook, or a 'big river pattern', or what? This stuff is important, if you want to kill birds. And we didn't kill any birds again today.

"You have to give ducks a good landing zone; an approach that's clear of decoys, especially when working both ducks and geese. You don't want birds having to have to fly over decoys, otherwise they'll move on, or land short of the decoys out of range."

Version #5: Decoys Too Spread

"Taylor sets decoys up in separate counties, more like separate *countries*. Not good. These birds *like* each other, like to stay together. That's why it's called 'flocking', duh.

"They'll bunch up during bad weather. We should have set our decoys much tighter than normal. No luck today."

Version #6: Too Many Decoys—Early Season[8]

"You don't need a big spread for these early birds. Lots of young birds, plus these birds haven't been shot at. You only need a couple of blocks[9] this early. But no, Ellis puts out every damned decoy he owns . . . that's a hell of a lot. Don't work this early in the

---

[8] "I'd say most hunters 'over decoy'. I've shot more birds over a half-dozen to a dozen decoys than over large spreads. It usually doesn't pay to use a large number." Dennis Ludington, Dog trainer and duck hunter, Volta Wildlife Refuge, California.

[9] 'Blocks' is a very cool synonym for 'decoys', in duck-hunterese.

season, and it's too much work for when it's this warm, anyway.

"Sometimes, I don't know why I put up with Ellis. Maybe because it's his blind, his property, his decoys, he brings the propane heater, the coffee, donuts and sandwiches, and an ample supply of 'Lynchburg Lemonade' . . . for after the hunt, of course.

"But never mind all that, Ellis still doesn't get it . . . still puts out too many dekes. Sometimes two decoys draws a hundred birds, and a hundred decoys won't draw two birds. It's all about how many to use *when,* and Ellis just doesn't get it. Early season, birds haven't been shot over, plus they haven't rafted up like later in the season.

"The birds don't like the look of a couple of hundred decoys. It's like the steak house downtown: nobody goes there anymore, 'cause it's too crowded. Ducks is the same way."

Version #7: Too Many Decoys—Late Season[10]

"This late in the season, you just don't need a set that big (pick one): out here.; down here.; over here.; up here.

"These birds don't like a big set. Late season birds are accustomed to large, unconvincing spreads. This late, they seen it all, believe me.

"Our big rig spooked those suspicious ducks, drove them to natural looking water holes. An old-timer in Maine once said, 'If you've got the right place, all you need is one.'

"Crenshaw, it's his idea to use dozens and dozens of dekes when we hunted that frozen corn field . . . ducks flew right on by.

"We're going back with just one damned decoy, our best 'smoothie' black duck . . . then we'll get those ducks, I promise you. No big late season spread this time."

---

[10] Rather than always using a large spread, try adding movement to a smaller decoy rig. From 'Discover the Outdoors.com'.

"Wait... Wait... Okay... Ready...
Now!"

Version #8: Danny Sets 'Em Wrong Again[11,12,13]

"Danny set the decoys wrong again. That boy is never going to get it right. There's a particular set for a particular time. It's another one of those right-wrong things . . . right set at the wrong time equals no ducks . . . wrong set at the right time means no ducks. Plus, Danny is *never* satisfied.

"First a 'cluster and slot', which I tell him from the get-go is wrong. Then a couple of ducks cross us about a mile high, and Danny's back changing things up to what he calls a 'bowl spread'.

"Well, we don't see ducks for about fifteen minutes and he's back at it. This time, Danny is working on what he calls a 'hybrid', some sort of mixture between a 'j' spread, a 'v' spread, and a 'fishhook'. Lord almighty, we're going *nuts*.

"Danny's fooling around again. This time, apparently changing to an 'hourglass' and, what do you know, in comes a dozen greenheads, locking up. As expected, they see Danny and split.

"Well, it figures. Danny is back and forth between the blind and the decoys all morning, alternating between a 'bowl spread', a 'swimming spread', and a 'scatter spread' . . . and every time birds swing by, Danny's out splashing and banging around, moving decoys every which damned way. Killed no ducks this morning . . . surprise, surprise."

---

[11] MIT and the CalTech have received grants to study the "Decoy Set Wrong" phenomenon, $78 million to MIT, and $44 million to Cal Tech. (Which seems a pittance to any serious duck hunter.)

[12] Refer to my six volume edition, *Decoys: A Treatise on Science, Art and Nature Integrating with Hunters and Ducks. Who Will Prevail?* 916 pages. Stinky Dog Press (www.whatisthatsmell.com) or Amazon.com. This oeuvre is an indispensable companion edition to my first book, *Optimal Decoy Arrangements—Or How to Achieve Duck Hunting Success While Keeping Your Friends' Mouths Shut.*

[13] "First, put out ten mallard decoys. If they're needed and the spot is good, then the rest of the decoys can go out. In the dark, it's hard to resist the temptation to put all the decoys out, but it pays to wait." Fletcher, p.21

Version #8: Forgot the Bodies

"We tote ten sacks all the way into the middle of the field . . . still an hour before dark. We open the sacks and they're all *heads!* Billy Ray has decoys with the detachable heads, he puts them in separate sacks, he forgets the sacks with the bodies—so all we got is long necked heads. Imagine how we did. Lousy, that's how. What self-respecting goose will come into a bunch of heads, eh? Darn, instead of being like the 'headless horseman', it was like the 'horseless headman.'"

Version #9: Forgot the Heads[14]

"We tote the sacks way out into the field . . . still an hour before dark. We open the sacks and they're all *bodies!* Billy Ray has decoys with the detachable heads and puts them in separate sacks and he forgets the heads—so all we got is bodies with no necks, no heads. Look like clumps of you-know-what, they did. Imagine how we did. Lousy, that's how. What self-respecting goose will come into a bunch of Anne Boelyn decoys?'"

Version #10: Competitors Have Robo-Ducks[15]

"The other guys had a Robo Duck, Mojo Duck, Lucky Duck, something. The birds just worked their way, then dropped right in on them. We got to get one of those things before they outlaw them."

---

[14] "To some, the authenticity of their decoys is important. I am not among them. I have seen too many ducks come hurtling in to spreads improvised from heaps of mud or seaweed, and to stools of floating oil cans. I have watched too many ducks flare and veer away from flotillas of artistically fashioned decoys. I am convinced that the willingness or reluctance of ducks to decoy is governed by psychological factors within the birds themselves, factors beyond the power of the gunner to influence one way or the other." Janes, p. 73.

[15] Technically, these are 'spinning wing' decoys. Arkansas banned decoys defined as "any electronic, mechanically-operated, wind-powered or manually-powered spinning-blade device that simulates wing movement,"

Version #11: Robo-Ducks Outlawed[16]

"What are those game Commissioners thinking? We've killed our last duck, I know that. Without one of those mechanical ducks, it'll be just like it was—no ducks. They say we're taking too many young ducks, but you couldn't prove that by me. If you listen to Fish & Wildlife, it's like we're shooting them in the eggshell. Folks say it's more ethical to use plain decoys, but then why don't we just give up decoys and shoot birds with a b.b. gun . . . that'd be plenty ethical, wouldn't it?"

"This baby will really bring 'em in. It's our new Super Mag RX decoy, and for 36 easy payments of..."

---

[16] Current restrictions on electronics devices cannot prevent the development of new hunting technologies that may have negative effects on waterfowl. Fair chase is also an issue with the potential to diminish the core value of quality duck hunting." The Concerned Ducks Hunters Panel.

JOHNSON

Boats and Equipment[1,2]

Version #1: Hit a Sunken Stump

"Hit a stump on the way out, we did. Nothing much you can do. It's pitch black at that time of the morning. Henry was supposed to be looking for stumps. Instead, he's back fooling with his stuff, bitching and moaning about his coffee leaking all over his shells, when "wham!" we hit a stump good. Everything goes flying out; there's a dent and a crack in the metal; and damned if we didn't have to go back in. No ducks today . . . thanks to Henry, that is. And, we still gotta go back and get our stuff off the bottom . . . maybe in July."

Version #2: Burned Up the Outboard Motor

"Randy, as usual, forgot to check the oil. We get a piece of trash, maybe a garbage bag, wrapped around the prop. And Randy starts running that motor fast as he can, without pulling it out to see what's the problem. Next, the motor burns up and we have to paddle all the

---

[1] "Boats play so prominent a role in most hunting trips that they can be considered an integral part of the gunner's equipment." Janes, p. 83.

[1] "Duck hunting is the most complicated and complex kind of hunting, a distinction at least from the point of view of the variety and amount of gear necessary to carry it on. We, with our galaxies of gadgets are presented with almost infinite opportunities to misuse them and perpetuate a variety of Damn Fool Things." MacKenty, p. 154.

way back in. You can wear a bunch of Mossy Oak™, but with no boat, you're SOL."

Version #3: Leaky Boat

"We push Caleb's fourteen foot leaky aluminum v-hull down to the river, using my new nine horsepower outboard. Caleb said his boat had a little leak. Little leak, my ass. More like the Grand Coulee Dam with turbines running full out. I made the guys turn around. That, or we'd have swum back home."

Version #4: Shooting from a Canoe

"I knew Bob hunted, but I never knew how, so when he asked me to go, well, I said 'sure'. Then he takes me out and we load up in a canoe . . . it's tipping like crazy . . . only one guy can shoot. The whole time I was petrified that we were going into that water. I didn't *want* to kill any ducks, I just wanted to *go in*. If I had known we were going to hunt from a canoe, I'd have slept in."

Version #5: Mike Flipped the Boat[3]

"I told him, the decoys are fine, but that boat is really unstable. Does Mike ever listen? Nooooooooo. Standing up, long pole in hand, trying to hook a decoy line . . . he was all set to go. I'm just glad the water wasn't that cold . . . it was only thirty degrees or so."

---

[1] "Police rescued a Lake Ronkonkoma man after his boat overturned while duck hunting in Bellport Bay. According to Suffolk County police, 24-year-old Michael Mandello was retrieving decoys about 9:35 a.m. when high winds overturned his 15-foot aluminum duck boat, throwing him into 37-degree water. Officers pulled him out and brought him to a waiting ambulance at the Smith Point Marina. Authorities said Mandello was not wearing a life jacket. According to Coast Guard statistics, boaters face the highest risk of dying during winter months. The window of opportunity for rescue is only a few minutes if the person is not dressed for the conditions. Nearly 90% of boating fatalities are due to drowning and half of those are attributed to immersion in cold water." NEWSDAY.COM, January 16, 2006

"Hey, anyone can shoot a hole in a boat!"

"Yeah, there's gonna be some good eating today."

Bad Hunters[1,2]

Whatever the description, 'bad hunters' will ruin a lot of duck hunts. The two essential archetypes in the genre are:

a. Friends who hunt with you, share your blind: They're not bad hunters, just 'great guys who had a little bad luck'. Therefore, when with you, they transform into 'good' hunters, though sometimes too exuberant.

b. Those you do not know, but somehow got the blind next to yours, referred to as 'those a-holes over there', 'just plain bad hunters', or 'those guys that somebody ought to do something about some day.'

It is no small distinction that bad hunters who are not friends would, in fact, be friends, if you were actually hunting with them, making the 'bad hunters' into good guys and simultaneously just unlucky hunters, not bad hunters. Got it?

Similarly, your friends, if hunting elsewhere—summarily become 'a-holes', and 'people that somebody should someday do something about.'

Basically, just remember that bad hunters make for a bad duck

---

[1] "One had a cannon and was shooting at everything within 100 yards, continually standing up in the open. We knew from experience that our neighbors would have a tough time killing ducks from their spot. Things weren't any better when they shot three white front geese which were out of season." Fletcher. P. 73.

[2] "My hunt ended when a sky busting hunter in the next field crippled a big honker which led my dog, and therefore me, on a big chase." Fletcher, p. 65

hunt, wherever they are and whoever they are. Very simple. Oh, and one more rule to remember: It's never you who is the 'bad hunter'.

Version #1: Sky Busting[3, 4]

"There's nothing worse than your neighbor sky busting. You sit there all day, finally get some birds working, and all of a sudden, blam, blam, blam. Two seconds later, there's not a thing in the sky, except a few starlings. Ninety percent of hunters say over fifty yards is sky busting. A guy will kill a duck by dumb luck at sixty or seventy yards, and for the rest of his life he's some damned Buffalo Bill and Annie Oakley, combined. At least in *his* mind. He'll tell that story a hundred times, but no one ever hears the stories about how he crippled so many ducks and ruined duck hunting for other guys. Today was like that. No ducks again today, duh."

---

[3] "The key is getting the right spot, then waiting for the nearly point-blank shot." Fletcher, p. 51 (The author agrees. After all, if you can do this, why worry about all the other stuff?)

[4] "Public areas are especially subject to sky-busting. No one yet has found a remedy. It's a handicap with which you'll have to live, don't count on working swing birds without adjacent blinds having a crack at them." Hinman, p. 193.

Other Great Excuses

Ambushing[1,2,3]

"Louie says he has a goose field, would I like to come hunt? He has driven around, scoped out a number of places, talked to the local rice farmers and gotten permission to hunt. Sure, I say. Well, he's got a field—that's all he's got. No decoys, no pit, no blind. This'll be great, he says. We'll creep up on them, then jump up and fire.

"I probably lost twenty pounds, trying to ambush geese. Maybe one time we got within three hundred yards. Mud sticking to your boots, wearing chest waders, sweating . . . worst hunting day ever."

---

[1] "The Ambush is a little foray into the Realm of the Ill-Conceived Plot. You think you can get close enough to a flock of geese for an all-out, wader-flopping, eye-bulging, Pickett-up-Cemetery Ridge charge. I've tried this scheme, and it ain't easy." Smith, p. 54.

[2] "[Ambushing] is the most difficult because it demands a skill, coordination and stamina far beyond that requisite in ordinary shooting." Janes, p. 31.

[3] "Sometimes it is possible to creep down wind within a hundred yards of the birds. When near enough, the gunner springs to his feet and runs toward them as fast as he can. As the birds must rise against the wind, they will sometimes come directly toward him before turning away." Grinnell, p. 277

"OK, so maybe there are a few tractor ruts out here."

Didn't Get Our Blind[4]

"Some guys got to our blind before us. They must've spent the night there. That's our area . . . I mean, even though it is public. We ended up in some godawful spot, and finally went in early without a bird."[5]

River Hunting's No Good[6]

"Past few years, river hunting's been no good. Used to have plenty on the river . . . sky was black with 'em . . . used to tear 'em up. But it's not like it used to be on the river."

Bay Hunting's No Good

"Past few years, bay hunting just hasn't been any good. No birds on the bay these days. We used to have plenty . . . sky was black with 'em . . . used to tear 'em up. But it's not like it used to be on the bay."

Not Enough Time

"No ducks today. F&W says that in the long-term average, there's not a lot of difference in the number of ducks . . . populations

---

[4] "Due to the migratory nature of ducks, unreliable water supplies, and variable crop harvests dates, alternative hunting locations are desirable." Fletcher, p. 82.

[5] "Open water, wind direction, and sun direction are the major considerations in selecting and setting up a blind." Fletcher, p. 76.

[6] "River shooting is practiced to great effect where narrow streams, flowing through deep beds, permit the gunner to walk along their winding course, and shoot ducks as they rise before him. In the South, river shooting is practiced by paddling along narrow streams, keeping close to the banks. In the narrow sloughs of Ohio, Illinois, Indiana and Minnesota, the same sport is practiced. Floating for ducks is likely to be practiced at any time in the spring or fall, but it is quite obvious that it is likely to be more successful in the early winter, after the quite ponds and slow-flowing sloughs are frozen." Grinnell, p. 341.

go up and down, year to year, but over decades it's relatively level. Well, I don't have decades to kill a damned duck. I'm not interested in averages. Heck, any man—an economist or a game warden—can still drown in a lake with an average depth of two feet. I want to kill a duck *today!*"

Sunspots[7]

"*USA Today* or one of those research-type newspapers said there's a lot going on with sunspots right now. All morning the ducks flared, and I got to conclude that it's the sunspots. In fact, the sun looked kind of funky this morning."

Need Odd Ducks

"We couldn't find the odd ducks needed to fill our limit. We'd get our mallards, then have to sit and wait for teal or gadwalls to finish up. Oh, yeah, and we didn't get any mallards either."

Fell in the Water[8]

"Okay, so Leo's putting decoys out, Dewitt is adding brush to

---

[7] *The Tectonic Strain Theory of Geophysical Luminosities* clearly establishes the cause-and-effect relationship between bad ducks hunts and sunspots. Under this theory, there are certain specific times of the year when sunspots will negatively affect duck and goose hunting, usually September through the middle of February in the Western Hemisphere. The Theory states, "Lunar and solar radiographic, magnetic, and light wave-length modulations have been shown to exert a negative influence on migratory animals of the Order *Anseriformes*, and in particular on the Family *Anatidae*, with respect to the ability of species Homo Sapiens' to lure such species within range of being able to slay or capture *Anseriformes Anatidae*."

[8] "Jim swings his gun and leans to one side. The dog thinks it a good time to get off the seat, and does it so expeditiously that with the report of the gun, both Jim and the ducks disappear, he having lost his balance by the recoil of the gun and Dan's untimely move. There is a resounding splash, and Jim's feet are hanging on the edge of the boat, while his body is in the water. This mishap spoiled our shooting." Grinnell, p. 350.

"Don't worry. . . I know where all
the stumps are."

the blind, Jacob is tying up the boat . . . well, it doesn't make any damned difference anyway, does it? Now, I know falling in is for beginners, but when you're hunting with those boys, anything can happen . . . and they managed to push me out of the boat. It felt kinda nice for about seven seconds, but at nine degrees, it gets uncomfortable pretty quick. No fire and no extra clothes, so I just sat in the blind until Jacob kept saying, 'Stand back . . . you're completely blue and you're flaring the ducks.' At that point I demanded to be taken back."[9]

Sun in Our Eyes[10]

"We got the only blind left, where the sun is directly in our faces, looking straight east. The only birds all morning came right out of the sun. Nobody saw them until its too late and they're gone."

Mud[11]

"Mud, mud, mud . . . delta gumbo. We couldn't move . . . we ended up taking hours just move anywhere, our guns got filthy. It was a mess getting in, getting back out, and keeping our stuff from getting covered."

---

[9] "Much later, a "friendly" hunter warned that great caution should be used when wading the ponds in the area, as some are quite deep." Fletcher, p. 61.

[10] "Orient the blind so that the morning sun will not hit you square in the eyes, and remember, as you build the blind—probably in October—that by December the sun will rise a lot further south than it did on Columbus Day." MacKenty, p. 12.

[11] "There existed a skim of ice, too thick to be pushed through with a boat, yet hardly strong enough to bear one's weight, there is a danger of wetting, if not of something worse: for the mud is deep and sticky, and he who is once mired in it will escape only with difficulty and discomfort." Grinnell, p. 242.

Shooting in the Woods[12]

"In the woods, the shooting is fast and furious. They're just hard to see in tall timber. They're on top of you before you realize it, so you have to decide in a split second if they're within range, if they're going to decoy, or if they should be taken on the pass.[13] We did lousy shooting in the woods today.

"Even though it's tricky to track, lead and shoot a bird before it's swallowed in the maze of branches, you'll take more birds if you stick exclusively to pass-shooting. Often, mallards that appear to be decoying will circle and then, spotting something out of place, disappear over the treetops."

Wrong Kind of Ducks[14]

"The day was a total bust. There were mallards and pintails everywhere and all we got was a merganser. If I'd wanted that, I could have gone fishing."

Wrong Gender

"Hens all day . . . hens, hens, hens. You'd think a self-respecting drake would wander by, wouldn't you? Sam says, 'Is this some kind of women's movement? I think I'm going to see Gloria Steinem fly by.'"

---

[12] Keith Sutton, *Arkansas Sportsman Magazine*

[13] "Of all methods of duck shooting, that known as pass shooting is perhaps the most difficult and the most sportsmanlike." Grinnell, p. 317.

[14] "Not sure what kind you've shot? Take it home and compare it with pictures in your duck book, or ask someone more expert than you are at identifying it." MacKenty, p. 158.

"Be careful now. . . it gets a little deep
up ahead."

Too Long a 'Sweat Line'[15]

"The sweat lines are way too long in (Cutter, Colusa, etc). There were a hundred trucks at four a.m., waiting for places from hunters that didn't show up. We sit all morning inching up the line, but nobody's leaving the marsh, so there's no spots before legal shooting time."

Hunting in the Tidewater

"Some Virginia locals took their Senator hunting in the Tidewater area. The Senator dropped a bird, but it fell into a farmer's field on the other side of a fence.

"Better go get him," the locals said, "can't leave a downed duck."

As the Senator climbed over the fence, an elderly farmer drove up on his tractor. "What're you doing?"

The Senator responded, "I shot a duck and it fell in this field. I'm just going into retrieve it."

The old farmer replied. "This is private property."

The Senator was indignant. "Do you know who I am?" he demanded.

"Don't make me no never mind who you are or who you're not," replied the farmer, "that duck is on private property."

"This is preposterous. It's only a few feet over the fence."

"Well," drawled the farmer, "seeing how that duck is so important, I'll tell you what. Let's settle it 'Tidewater Style' and just use the Virginny 'Three Kick Rule'.

"What's that?" asked the politician.

---

[15] 'Sweat Line' refers to hunters waiting for a spot to hunt in a public marsh on a first come, first served basis. The term is most frequently used in northern California (Colusa, Honey Lake, Gray Lodge, Sacramento, Merced, Delevan, Grizzly Island, Los Banos, San Luis, Sutter, Tule Lake, Lower Klamath, Kesterson, Modoc, Mendota, Ash Creek, Butte Valley and Volta.)

"Well, first I kick you three times, then you kick me three times, and we keep agoin' 'til somebody give up."

"The Senator assessed the short, skinny farmer, figuring he could take the old codger, and quickly agreed.

"The farmer slowly climbed down, walked up to politician, and planted the toe of his heavy work boot into the Senator's crotch, dropping him to his knees. His second kick nearly ripped the man's nose off. His third kick crushed into the Senator's ribs.

"The Senator, gasping for air and spitting up blood, barely managed to rise to his feet and gasp, "Okay you old geezer, now it's your turn."

The farmer grinned, climbed back on his tractor and, pulling away, said, "Naw, I give up. Go on and take your damned duck. Plus, this ain't my farm anyhow. I'm just cuttin' across."

Just "Little Ducks"[16]

"All we saw were damned little ducks, teal or something. We waited for big ducks, but they never did come. Never fired a shot."

Stuttgart[17,18]

"Stuttgart's just not what it used to be. We need to be out at Tule Lake or the Klamath Basin. Maybe Delevan, Colusa, or Sutter . . . Jimmie says you can hunt in a t-shirt, too. We oughta give some thought to moving West, like Henry Fonda in that movie where everyone is poor and stuff."

---

[16] "To shoot big ducks, one must kill a few less ducks at times. Often, big ducks won't come in until they see the other ducks working the area. Widgeon, teal and spoonbill become decoys that encourage the mallards and sprig. If the smaller ducks are shot, you'll never know what may have been," Fletcher, p. 51

"Today's recipe—Snow Goose Parmesan. First soak goose in battery acid for three days."

---

[17] Stuttgart, which calls itself the Duck Hunting Capital of the World. Stuttgart is the home of the World Championship Duck Calling Contest and offers some of the finest duck hunting in the world. The truth is, nothing is like it used to be . . . for example, the *earth*. By the way, that's another excuse for striking out, 'global warming'.

[18] In 1947, St. Louis Post-Dispatch editor Ralph Coghlan wrote: *I have never seen more ducks than darkened the Arkansas skies this year. Not being a bookkeeper, an accountant, a human adding machine or a member of the federal Fish and Wildlife Service, I couldn't come within 100,000 of figuring how many I saw. I watched mallards sitting in vast and solid rafts on the Arkansas reservoirs quacking raucously and happily, and at dusk, saw them start for the rice fields. They took off in successive roars like fleets of miniature B-29s, and for half an hour or more the whole sky was alive with ducks.*

THE USE OF
MULTIPLE EXCUSES

The Use of Multiple Excuses

*"*I*n summer, 1984 the drought in the Canadian prairies was in its fourth year. Pintail and mallard populations were dropping. Pothole counts were down drastically. Worse, Canadian farmers took advantage of the conditions to convert the dried potholes into wheat fields. Short grass prairie habitat essential for pintail nesting was being lost at a rate of 300,000 acres per year. The effect of high predation rates on nests and nesting hens in prairie Canada had become painfully evident. The future for pintails, in particular, appeared bleak."*

—California Waterfowl Association

Above is an example of combining weather, water, farmers, predation . . . some real good stuff. In order deliver a convincing excuse for striking out on a duck hunt, it is often necessary to mix and match excuses. Blaming several factors can carry enormous weight, even with veteran hunters who might otherwise suspect that you have no idea what the heck you are doing out there in the first place:

"Well, Freddie kept jumping in and out of the blind to arrange the stool, or personally create one of his own out in the weeds somewhere. Then, there weren't any ducks around, and if there had been, it wouldn't have made any difference because we got a lousy place this morning and there were bad hunters all around us using terrible calls."

Or: "With this hot and cold weather and the dry and wet spells we've had, you just can't find a duck. Even if you could, my boat is giving me trouble and I've got the wrong kind of decoys."

Or: 'It was too warm, the wind was wrong, decoys were set up wrong, Danny kept getting out of the blind to move his bowels, Bobby Rae kept looking up and flaring the ducks, there weren't any ducks, the boat sank, and we forgot our guns, shells, and the boat motor."

These simple examples demonstrate the awesomely persuasive power of combining multiple excuses. You'll never get good at excuse delivery until you try it, so jump in and convince your friends that absolutely none of it was your fault.

Lightning Source UK Ltd.
Milton Keynes UK
176972UK00002B/2/P